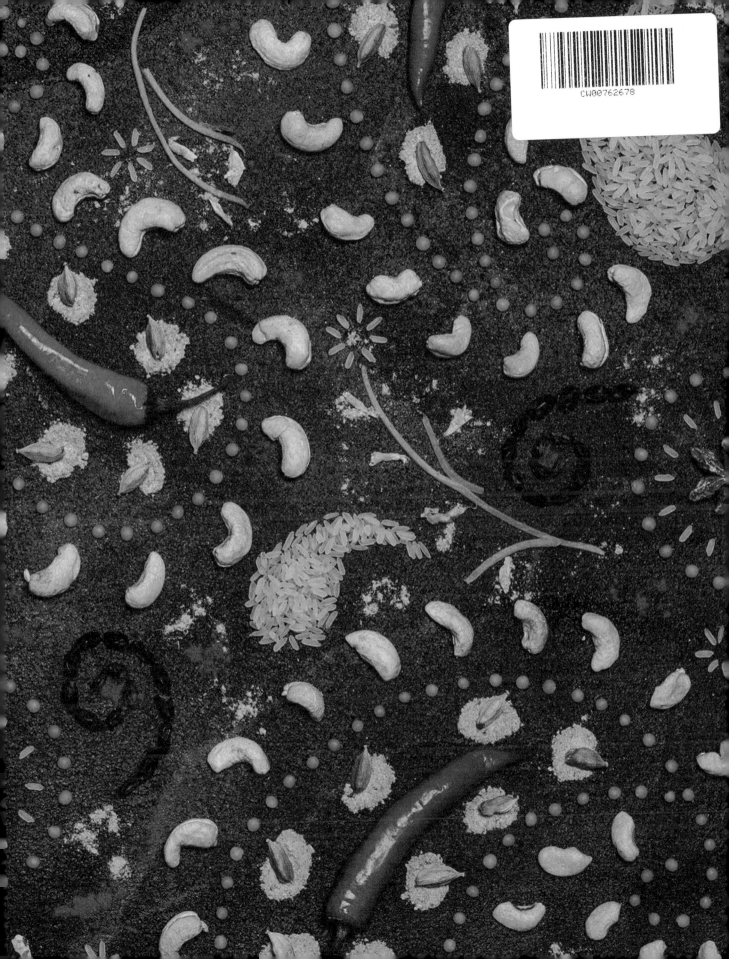

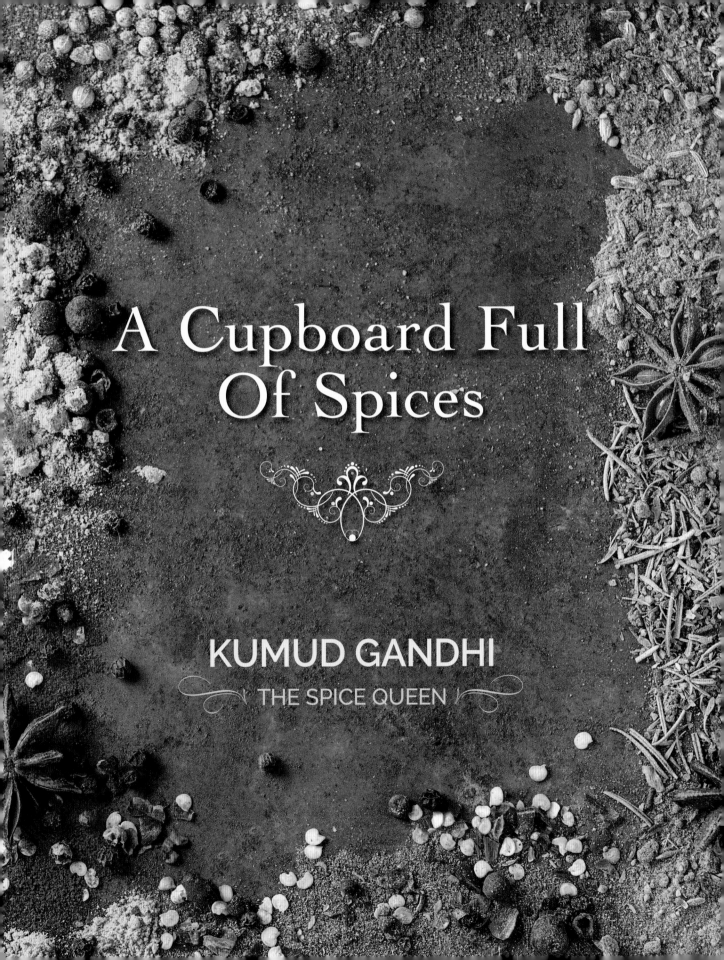

A Cupboard Full Of Spices

KUMUD GANDHI

THE SPICE QUEEN

First published in Great Britain in 2018

Text copyright © Kumud Gandhi 2018
Design & layout © Sam Pearce, SWATT Books Ltd.
Photography © Kumud Gandhi

ISBN 978-1-9164567-0-9

Printed and bound by Biddles Books Limited
Publisher: Kumud Gandhi
Designer: Sam Pearce, SWATT Books Ltd.
Photographer: Mel Johnson, Kumud Gandhi, Chloe Hickman
Home Economy: Mel Johnson, Sarah Leary, Kumud Gandhi
Food Styling: Mel Johnson, Kumud Gandhi

Endorsements for "A Cupboard Full of Spices"

"I love food but I particularly have a love of Indian food. Not much can beat a Chicken Jalfrezi for me with a cold beer and Kumud's book has opened me up to many other traditional Indian culinary delights. I love the way she puts so much love and joy into her recipes and they work 100%. Nothing can compete with a family all sitting together eating great food and laughing and this is precisely what her book encourages – cooking for family and friends.

The spice chapter really helps to put everything into context and it makes the recipes in this book so easy to understand. I have attempted many of them with a thumbs-up from my own very discerning family.

I hope you all enjoy this book as much as I have. Love and good food make the world go around. Thank you Kumud for this gift."

Aled Jones

"Kumud just *understands* spices and authentic flavours - and how to cook with them. Her food is always delicious, her recipes very easy to cook. She is so passionate about her heritage and loves sharing that via the food she cooks."

Nick Coffer
food writer and broadcaster

Acknowledgements

Writing this book has been an incredible experience with a range of emotions, from fond memories of my childhood, joy, laughter and indulgence right through to emotional hysteria and a gruelling photography schedule with my delightful support team. It has been a fantastic documentation of my food experiences from childhood through the years to the present day. Above all else it has been a labour of love and whilst that may sound clichéd, my recollections and writing journals throughout this process have been all about the love of food and life that has been shared on my journey.

The writing of this book has also enabled me to celebrate my father in the way I have known him the most, his passion for life, his spiritual beliefs and guiding light. My deepest acknowledgement goes to him for passing this spirit on to me, his joie de vivre. I thank him for sharing his joy, his wisdom, generosity of spirit, passion and of course his discerning palate. Thank you Papa.

I'd also like to thank my children, Savannah and Natalia, for embracing the third sibling, 'The Cooking Academy', and always being the hungry hippos, ready to test my recipes with brutal honesty. My thanks also goes to Hasruty, my counsel, my food buddie and partner in crime for indulging without guilt and ordering everything on the menu.

I have a special thank you to Sarah, my tour manager, sub-editor, and crazy cat lady for helping me bounce ideas around the kitchen; her support and encouragement have been unyielding. Paul for kicking my butt to get on with the book, mentoring me in his own inimitable style all the way from the French Alps. Collectively, they have all played a vital role in getting this book on the shelf.

Thank you for your kind words and kinship.

A Cupboard Full Of Spices

KUMUD GANDHI
THE SPICE QUEEN

My love of sharing food is a deep-seated passion from which I have discovered myself and my life's work. What could possibly be more satisfying than cooking for family and friends and sharing knowledge of food? It is truly a labour of love.

Contents

Author's Note

I grew up in a household where life seemed to revolve around the kitchen, so unsurprisingly the vast majority of my earliest memories involve food in one way or another.

It seemed to be the hub of the house and where all the most important decisions were made, and certainly where the answer lay to most questions. I would perhaps go as far as saying I think that it's the place where I learnt the most about life, whether it was from my siblings and their wildly exaggerated stories, or aunties recounting their rich tapestry of life. The kitchen was also the place where I learned to trust the yielding nature of herbs and spices and came to understand the circle of life and the importance of the seasons for nature to take its course organically.

It's also where my family shared generations of knowledge regarding spices and their specific benefits both for flavour and medicinally. It seemed that the spice cupboard held the answer before the physician! This sharing of Indian traditions, recipes, cooking secrets and tips for perfection is all I have known since my childhood and is probably what has led me to impart and share my knowledge through the cookery school.

Today the kitchen is the hub of my house and I suspect my children would say the same. I've probably felt the most relaxed and comfortable when cooking and preparing food for everyone to enjoy - family, friends and even strangers.

Writing a book about spices and recipes using the most appropriate and flavoursome spices has been a long journey. One which has been encouraged and nurtured by customers and friends of the cookery school alike, eager to have a reference point and compendium of knowledge at hand in their kitchens.

My book is about the journey of food and what it means to us, through history and its preparation. Food has a universal ability to connect us. As human beings we have a primal need to eat and this is my attempt to encourage you into the kitchen to cook recipes that have always been a part of my history and traditions.

What I want this book to do above all else is give pleasure!

The pleasure that comes from sharing food, cooking for others, the pleasure of discovering a new favourite ingredient, the pleasure of knowing that the food you are cooking is energizing and stimulating in both body and soul.

I want to share a deep and meaningful connection to the ingredients and the cooking techniques we use to nourish ourselves. I want you to take the information, recipes and tips in this book and run with them, experiment with both spices and herbs, occasionally have a complete disaster, forgive yourself and really grow in confidence as a cook. I want the profusion of overwhelming sensations and flavours to make you say 'wow'.

I want this book to sit on your shelf, dog-eared from use, the odd smear of sauce throughout and the pages of your favourite recipes stuck together from over-eager leafing. I'd like you to feel exhilarated by the fantastic things food can do for our health and wellbeing, and excited about putting that knowledge to good use in the kitchen and sharing that experience with others. It is time to start reacquainting ourselves with the power of food to empower and nourish us. We hear so much about the damaging effects of processed food with high sugar and salt content and the impact this has had on two

generations of people, with obesity and the rise of type 2 diabetes. Therefore, this book is about giving you the good news: a way to create tasty and delicious recipes using ingredients that are actually beneficial to your health. I want you to take time to have fun and really enjoy cooking and when you do that, you will develop an ability to cook with all of your senses, and engage with it lightheartedly but wholeheartedly, **because food is a sensual experience.**

The fast pace of life can often make food a 'pit stop': practical or even gratuitous comfort food, rather than nurturing and yielding. 'Heart and soul' cooking is about using all of your senses; you want to be able to hear the cooking processes sizzling, smell the changes in the aroma, feel the texture as you cook, taste the flavours you are creating and see the colours as they unfold in front of you. **This is what I call cooking with your heart.**

Good, wholesome food and its preparation are a source of timeless pleasure and fun. It is not just about the eating, but rather the whole experience, thinking about the menu, shopping for the ingredients, cooking it, talking about it and finally sitting down with others to savour every mouthful. When you cook like this, you

are surrendering something of yourself in each mouthful.

The recipes I have selected from my extensive back catalogue are all simple to re-create and are the kind of dishes eaten by Indian families on a daily basis. Some of them have been in my family for over 100 years and it is a privilege to share them with you.

This collection is an unapologetic desire to celebrate food and its virtues. My recipes are a feast of bold colours (like India itself) and generosity of spirit. Don't be put off by what might seem like a long list of ingredients; once you understand the simple methods involved and the spicing process, you'll see what a pleasure it can be to cook Indian food from scratch.

My Early Years

We all have a complex relationship with what we eat, which is wrapped up in our family history.

It's never too late to change our eating habits to experience something new and exciting. For some, food is consumed to provide energy, but for me food is about life itself, a celebration of culture, virtues and ideology; and most of all, food is about bringing people together, hearts and minds, united by a need to eat.

Originally from India, my parents emigrated to the UK in the 1950s. My father was a passionate foodie with one of the most discerning palates I have ever known. His ability to recognize flavours and decipher how to improve a recipe was quite something. I vividly recall my mother checking every dish before serving a meal to ensure it would meet with his approval.

I can barely remember a single moment when our kitchen wasn't abuzz with people and the aromas of whatever was cooking on the stove that day. The menu would be decided the night before and preparation would even start before breakfast, with the soaking of lentils or sifting of rice. Rice was bought in sacks and stocked up for the year ahead as rice improves with age.

Roped in to help from an early age, it was my job to transfer the rice from the hessian sacks to large storage drums and I can still smell the hessian now. The empty sacks would then be used as beanbags for our recreation – practising for the school sports day sack race!

I was also enlisted to help tend to our herb garden, sowing the coriander and fenugreek seeds, watering them and looking after them until finally revelling in the satisfaction of picking the fully-grown crop and preparing it for supper. My favourite was cress from mustard seeds, a delightful peppery taste that would stimulate my taste buds and leave a really refreshing and reviving flavour. Of course, I didn't know at that time that there's more to mustard than its potent taste as it's also a powerful liver tonic and a strong vitamin C agent.

In the summer months, under my father's supervision, we would head down to the seafront and forage for samphire, a delicate sea vegetable that is incredibly rich in taste and texture, rich in vitamins A, B and C. Others would be curious about our finds and question how one might cook them. Today, you will often see samphire appearing on the menus of top restaurants, but in those days you couldn't even buy it in the shops. These experiences have left me with a nostalgic adoration for the food from my childhood, what I consider to be 'real' Indian food, packed with fresh fruit and muddy vegetables with natural earthy minerals.

We also indulged in traditional British fare, making use of an abundance of local-grown apples and blackberries for warming pies, crumbles and chutneys.

I took fresh, local ingredients for granted and this has had a huge influence on my cooking and my love of gardening.

I try to keep food as natural as possible and avoid complicated cooking methods wherever I can. By keeping things simple and unfussy, you maintain the freshness of the dish. Each ingredient has a clear voice and even though Indian cuisine has an abundance of spices and flavours, you should still be able to taste every element. The best Indian food is a world away from the often sloppy and over-spiced takeaway curries you'll find on the high street.

Looking back further, there are generations of spice merchants and chemists in my family tree, perhaps explaining the roots of my scientific approach to food. As a child, I was lucky enough to travel throughout South East Asia and I usually spent my summers in India basking in the sun, picking local ingredients and spending hours with my aunties and great aunties, whilst they explained all the weird and wonderful vegetables to me. As an inquisitive child, my questions were patiently answered and these intimate moments have always stayed with me. But it took a while before I could make my life's passion my life's work.

Before I founded The Saffron House catering company and The Cooking Academy, I had worked in the corporate world of banking and finance, which came with great opportunities of travel to some wonderful food destinations, particularly in Asia and the Middle East with all the exotic herbs and spices that make those parts of the world such gastronomic havens.

This is where I began to develop a sense of what I had taken for granted up until then, that my understanding of food was great and my desire to learn more needed to be fulfilled. It wasn't until I took a career break to have my children that I understood just how much more there was to learn about food and just how much it engaged my own passions in life.

Whilst making baby food for my children and experimenting with different methods of preservation I stumbled upon the concept of 'Food Science' at the London Food Centre.

They were essentially providing the analysis and method behind the chemistry of food, validating all the Ayurvedic remedies I had experienced throughout my childhood. And whilst I had never doubted their validity, the fact that I could demonstrate the science behind the theory excited me immensely. Before too long I found myself enrolling on a course, super excited about piecing together the jigsaw puzzle I had sixty percent of the pieces to. My formal food journey began here, I suppose, and whilst I thought I was studying for my own curiosity and pleasure

I had no idea what lay in wait for me. Not only did I learn so much more about the food farming and agricultural process but also about the nutritional value and the long-term effects on the human frame.

It cemented my understanding of the relationship between the chemistry of food and the impact on our human biology. My studies gave me the opportunity to experiment with ingredients and test recipes in a variety of ways. My knowledge of ingredients and their structure gave me far greater confidence and I learned to 'play with food' which gave me a deeper connection to food. I immersed myself in a new perspective whilst still using the lovely exotic herbs and spices that I had grown up with as well as lots of exciting new ones.

It was during this time whilst I was a full-time mum and studying that I met such a wide range of people with diverse food interests, whether they were professionals, or foodies with a passion for entertaining. I was asked on several occasions to cater for dinner parties and though I hadn't ever considered such a career the personalities and clients were very interesting and I soon found myself drawn into a world of event catering for fashion and TV as well as the celebrity world quite by accident. Armed with my study of food science, my

particular understanding of spices from my family background as well as my own cooking experiences, I set about with energy and gusto to share my knowledge and palate with others.

I have had the distinct honour of cooking for Gywneth Paltrow and Chris Martin, the Prince of Wales, the Oxford Union, President of Iraq, Mayor of London, Tony Blair's office, and P. Diddy.

About the Cookery School

When I took a career break I hadn't started out thinking I wanted to run a cookery school. I wouldn't have imagined myself having the patience to teach.

However, like most things I suppose it evolved from my love of food and my love of sharing food with others, a deep desire that others should enjoy the same depth of flavours I find in food and be able to re-create them themselves. I also felt that I wanted to change the perception that Indian food is difficult to cook as many people seem to struggle to balance the flavours of this cuisine in particular.

In 2007 I set up The Cooking Academy with a mission to start passing on what I'd learned and passionately believe in. I was determined to get the message out there, that from the womb to our final hour – 'we are what we eat'. It's like most things in life; you get back what you put in, so by nurturing yourself with the right food, you will reap the benefits.

I wanted to share my understanding of food science and spices in a practical and easy to follow manner. I wanted to communicate just how easy it is to use herbs and spices to benefit one's health and improve wellbeing. I also wanted to share my recipes and philosophy on cooking, which is to open the cupboards or fridge and cook in a relaxed frame of mind; to not take yourself too seriously and make cookery a lifelong journey. Most of all I wanted to create a food community which is a wonderful thing to be a part of.

Mostly I felt that I wanted people to feel at ease with ingredients, particularly spices, not to be daunted by the idea of working with an array of different flavours and unfamiliar ingredients, but rather indulge in them and treat them like tiny pieces of treasure to use sparingly and to enjoy the outcome of what they had created.

The world is such a small place and the idea was to make it even smaller and more accessible, to create a 'global village' of food, culture and stories of one's experiences that could be shared with one another. I wanted such a class to be an engaging experience, one where learning would be fun, creative and convivial and so the surroundings had to be that of a domestic setting rather than a soulless

intimidating stainless steel industrial kitchen. People learn best when they are fully relaxed.

And so today we teach people how to prepare and cook food from around the world in a professional, enthusiastic and enjoyable way. We are unique in our approach to cookery by putting ingredients and their beneficial health properties at the heart of everything we teach.

The classes are entirely hands-on and taught by expert chefs using ethically sourced ingredients. Our ethos is to explain the chemical composition, Ayurvedic and herbal values of food so that recipes are nutritionally rich, look visually appealing and taste divine.

Our cookery classes change our students' perspective of food with a teaching methodology that makes no assumptions of their starting position. Instead we take them by the hand on a journey of discovery, peppered with lots of hints and tips to give a technical understanding of why certain processes are necessary in cooking to broaden one's knowledge.

We give our students the confidence to replicate our recipes at home and enable them to 'tweak' the dishes to their own palate.

We now teach over 3,000 students a year and it's a thrill to see them buoyed up with knowledge and enthusiasm for all kinds of wonderful herbs and spices after a day spent in the kitchen. So many of them come back again and again to continue their journey, because they understand the recipes and value the simple techniques and principles for everyday cooking.

Over the years I have made many amazing friends from around the world with whom I know I can share a plate. The one thing we have in common is our love of food.

Some come with very little experience; others have been cooking for decades and simply want to expand their repertoire or just have a great day out. Whatever their reasons for coming, I can confidently say they leave feeling inspired by their journey through the spice trail.

Read on, and I hope you too will derive just as much pleasure from your journey of curiosity along the spice trail as you learn about their plentiful benefits.

Herbs & Spices

Thousands of years ago in Ancient Greece...

Philosopher and physician Hippocrates, the father of medicine, said 'let food be thy medicine and medicine thy food' and this is the abiding principle by which I think about food. Hippocrates, the founding father of modern medicine, documented the link between food, our diet and our health. So the idea that eating certain types of food can have a positive effect on our wellbeing is not a new one.

Theophrastus, the Greek scholar, and botanists wrote treatises on medicinal plants including spices. And in recent years, doctors have been looking at our diet to find the answers to ailments and diseases such as diabetes, cancer and Alzheimer's. Not a day goes by without the national press reporting on another food group documenting scientific studies and bodies of evidence of exactly the same notion, **that food has healing properties.**

In the Indian system of natural medicine, Ayurveda, food plays an absolutely pivotal role in our wellbeing and practitioners go one step further by examining our body types to suggest the most appropriate diet to suit one's individual biochemistry, rather than the 'one-size fits all' approach. Similarities can be found in traditional Chinese medicine as well as in the Aztecs of South America.

Cultures all over the world have relied upon the naturally occurring chemical properties of herbs, spices and natural foods for their wellbeing long before the invention of modern science as we know it today.

The History of Herbs & Spices
– Where Did It All Start?

Herbs and spices are the very essence of nature that can be used to create delicate flavours and become the building blocks of a tasty dish.

As well as exciting the palate, they are made up of an impressive list of essential oils, phytonutrients, antioxidants, vitamins and minerals that are essential for overall health. Spices have been an integral part of our food for centuries. Today, with our busy, somewhat stressful lifestyles, it's never been more relevant to harness the goodness of nature to improve our wellbeing.

Humans have probably used spices in one form or another since we first began to cook with fire. After all, spices are just the seeds of naturally occurring trees and plants. Such plants were wild and grew like hedgerows, commonly available to all.

The use of spices is so ubiquitous; it is difficult to tell exactly where spices originate. The most commonly used spices originate from the East, India and South East Asia. The most notable exceptions to this are chillies, allspice and vanilla that come from the New World, Mexico and the Caribbean. A number of common culinary herbs are imports from the Mediterranean

and North Africa, discovered by the ancient Romans, Greeks and Persians; think of thyme, rosemary and coriander as examples. The movement of spices began over 5,000 years ago, long before the expeditions of Marco Polo and Columbus, where the travellers of the Middle East and Egypt were fascinated by the medicinal and culinary value of spices and were keen to take these from India back to their own lands. Ancient scripture has traced this practice back to 3000 BC.

The ancient Egyptians and Syrians were using spices for embalming and preservation and so this technique spread throughout the Middle East. Conquerors like Alexander the Great were well known for their interest in spices and the commercial enterprises they brought to Central and Northern Europe.

There is early evidence of pepper being used to aid the preservation of meats and to combat stomach pain. Right from the early days of travellers and tradesmen, the original Arab spice route from Northern and Southern India through the Khyber Pass into Persia (what is now the Middle East) and on to Europe and the rest of the world, we have been exchanging spices and learning about their valuable contributions to our civilization. One most fascinating fact is that the Americas may not have been discovered by the Europeans until much later, were it not for the European desire (Columbus) to break the Arab traders' monopoly on spices – an interesting thought!

The traders of the Middle East were the brokers for spices, essentially a gateway between the East and West. One could argue that the Arabs were the first truly global traders and power brokers. The key players were the Northern Arabians, who sent caravans and ships to India, China and Indonesia.

Meanwhile, here in Europe demand for spices grew significantly; the very wealthy bought spices like nutmeg and even paid a ransom in spices. This increasing demand enabled prices to remain high and spices to be considered very rare and a premium commodity. Much of the trade in India originated from the Malabar coast in Kerala, and also the Tamil region of India.

The Principal Use of Spices

In modern day Western Europe and the USA, flavour is the most commonly perceived reason for using spices.

Throughout the ages, spices have held three functions in cooking: medicinal, as a preservative and for seasoning. Each spice has a chemical property, a characteristic, as well as a taste. By knowing the composition of your spices you can begin to weave them into your everyday recipes. For example, ginger is clean and warm in character, medicinally; it is antibacterial and a digestive aid, whilst in taste it is hot and citrusy.

In the days before refrigeration, spices were also used as a means of preserving foods. The amazing longevity of Egyptian artefacts was achieved by embalming with spices; these have stood the test of time and lasted several millennia. In Middle Ages Britain, salt was predominantly used as a means of preserving meats; only the wealthy households used black pepper as it was very expensive. Since the taste of salt was so strong they used spices to try to balance the flavours in an attempt to disguise the saltiness.

Sauces were made to accompany the meat using spices such as cinnamon, star anise, saffron, garlic and nutmeg; and so began the use of spices in European food.

Great food is all about ying and yang, the fine balancing of sweet, sour, hot, salty and umami. When you harmonise the flavours correctly, you excite every part of your palate. Therefore in my cookery classes at The Academy, I talk a lot about the use of herbs and spices and how they pair intuitively. There are a number of ingredients that can be added to lift flavours to another level, for example adding lemon or tamarind to a chicken or fish dish at the end of the cooking process.

Balancing flavours is most important; no one flavour should dominate a dish, and in Asian food this is almost always achieved through the spicing or garnishing process. In vegetarian dishes where there is tartness, you would almost always add an element of sweetness to remove the sharpness of the tart ingredient. In dishes such as chicken, lamb or fish the sweetness of the meat would be rounded off with a dash of fresh lemon, chaat masala, or even garam masala.

When we know the broader context of spices we can begin to place their value and expand our use of them. We begin to open up the idea of cross fertilization and can experiment with a greater confidence that the outcome is likely to yield success and so is worth taking the risk of using it.

We know that cinnamon adds sweetness; star anise adds a liquorice flavour and sits well with fish dishes. Black pepper adds heat, but it is the chemical, piperine, in black pepper that adds both pungency and intensity to the dish, so elevates the flavour once again.

Definition of a Spice

My attempt to explain a spice is not solely based on a dictionary definition, but rather a logical deconstruction of the physical plant and its use in cooking.

A spice is obtained from the dried fruiting body of a plant, so it can be the whole fruit such as black pepper, allspice berries or cumin etc. In addition, a spice is also the kernel or seed of the fruit, as with nutmeg and fenugreek seeds or onion seeds.

In contrast, herbs are the vegetative parts of a plant (the stems and leaves) and include lemongrass, thyme and oregano leaves. One exception to this rule is the dried methi leaves (which are the dried leaves of the fenugreek plant) which are generally considered as a spice, since they are usually used in a dry form.

Furthermore, the roots and bark of plants in their dried form are also considered as spices. Just as turmeric and wasabi are since they are both derived from roots, so is cinnamon bark. By definition, a spice should not be perishable and can be preserved for many months with little loss of pungency if stored correctly.

Masalas

Masala is a commonly used term in Indian cooking and it literally translates to 'a blend of spices'; these are added to other herbs such as garlic or ginger and ground together to form the foundation of a sauce.

A wet masala is ground in a mortar or the modern day equivalent – a food processor (don't be alarmed; a Magimix is perfectly fine!). Liquids like oil, lemon juice, vinegar or yoghurt can be added during the grinding process to create a smooth and harmonious blend. You could also add nuts, coconut or onion to provide texture and viscosity. This masala is then used as a marinade or cooked in oil to enable the release of flavour before adding the main ingredients.

When it comes to the use of spices there are no hard and fast rules. I can't say that any one spice cannot work with another or that it will create discourse in the flavour however there are very basic guidelines. Turmeric, coriander, cumin and pepper have strong and bitter flavours so are added to savoury dishes that can withstand such intensity. On the other hand, saffron, cardamom and cinnamon are commonly used for desserts such as halva or rice puddings. In India, these spices tend to be winter favourites since they bring warmth to the northern, colder regions.

Getting to Know Your Spices

Spices have taste classifications such as sweet, sharp or pungent. Using some of the basic spices in the palate here are some examples:

1. Sweet yet subtly warm spices include: cinnamon, cardamom, nutmeg, cloves
2. Sharp and hot spices include: chilli powder, black pepper, garam masala
3. Pungent flavour enhancing spices include: coriander, cumin, fenugreek, and asafoetida

The great thing about spices is that different flavours can be extracted from the same spice by using different forms or methods of cooking, like grinding, roasting, sautéing, tempering, adding the whole spice, or ground spice or by combining the spice with other spices. For example whole cumin seeds will impart a different flavour to that of ground cumin. Furthermore, if the cumin seeds have been roasted prior to grinding, they too will impart a different flavour to the dish.

When you are experimenting, like most other experiments, only change one variable at a time to ensure you know how you have created the new flavour, or know the individual taste of your spices very well to decipher which spice has created the change.

Whichever spices you're using, they should not have disparate flavours, or taste raw (which is why spices are always layered into a dish and I shall come back to this point later on). No one spice should overpower the other and be so intrusive as to completely hide the true taste of the vegetable or meat being cooked. Instead, it should complement, maintain and enhance the character of the dish, giving it colour and fragrance and leaving you wanting more!

I like to think of this interrelationship as 'The Spice Palette'. Think of the individual spices being like the colours on an artist's palette; by mixing them the artist can generate different colours, shades and tones that in turn make up the whole picture. Similarly utilizing the spices enhances the expression, style and skill of the cook.

The spice tin is essentially your painting palette; the palette need not be as vast as you might think. There are a few principal spices, let's call them primary colours, required to get the process started. The key is to understand how a particular spice can affect your dish. Tasting the spices individually, in their raw state, is imperative. If you taste the spice and let the flavours permeate on your tongue you will be able to understand its contribution to the overall dish and make a judgement of its function, suitability and quantity – 'get to know your spices'.

Once you have done that, it is a question of arranging them in the recipe to achieve the flavour and balance required. In my classes, I also use a musical analogy: it is rather like learning the sound of each note of the piano keyboard; think of the spices as a note on the keyboard. Then you play a chord, acquaint yourself with each note and build your recipe. Once you have established a harmony you can fine-tune it, and before you know it your dishes will sing with flavour.

Understanding the Properties of Your Spices

Spices are split into two categories in the cooking process: whole spices and seeds, and ground spices.

When making sauce-based dishes you start with whole spices for the early infusion process. This is also referred to as a tempering, tarka or 'vaghar', where the spices are infused in hot oil or fat to release their essence and transfer the flavour from the spice to the oil. The oil is effectively a carrier that will distribute the flavour throughout the whole dish as you begin to add more and more ingredients to the pan.

Fat or oil is of paramount importance to the release of the volatile and essential oils in the spices, therefore it is important that you use oil and that it's used in sufficient quantity so that the spices can rehydrate and come to the fore to work properly and release their flavours.

Before you start cooking, think about what ingredients and spices you are going to use and which oil will be most suitable. In Indian cooking I would recommend a plain and simple oil such as rapeseed oil since it doesn't have any lingering flavours of its own and works well at high temperatures without damaging its nutritional value. However, sometimes it's worth using an oil such as peanut or mustard to accentuate the flavour of a dish.

Mustard oil has a very distinct flavour and when used with a pan-fried fish dish, let's say, it can really bring out the flavours. Or, for example, with a dish such

as jhaal muri, a popular chaat dish where the mustard oil will really enhance the flavours by permeating into the jhaal muri spice blend. Peanut oil is a light and tasty oil that can work well with green vegetables, often helping to take away the bitterness of spinach or okra. Peanut oil will also work well in stir-fries or a phad Thai and is commonly used in Thai and Chinese cooking.

A great way to intensify the flavours of the whole spices would be to toast them very lightly in a dry pan first, for just about a few seconds on a gentle heat. Set them aside in the pan, add the oil to the pan and once the oil is hot return the toasted spices to create a deep aroma. The oil should be hot but not smoking at the point at which you add them; cold oil will make them languish and retain the flavour within the seed for too long rather than imparting the flavours.

The fundamentals of your 'whole spice' tin for a sauce-based dish should probably start with cinnamon bark, cloves, cardamom – green and black, star anise, black pepper and bay leaves. They form the primary palette for the oil infusion.

If you are making a dry dish using vegetables or a stir-fry then it is likely that you will sauté seeds in hot oil rather than use whole spices. As stated earlier, this tarka or vaghar process, depending on what part of India you come from, it is when you sauté either whole spices, seeds or chillies in hot oil and then add other seasonings such as asafoetida or curry leaves followed by the main ingredient.

This is where your second spice tin will come in. It should contain all the most popular seeds and ground spices you are most likely to use. I would recommend you populate it with the two most widely used seeds, brown/black mustard seeds and cumin seeds, followed by the five most commonly used spices and flavour bedfellows, ground coriander, ground cumin, hot chilli powder, turmeric and garam masala.

Most other spices are used in selected recipes such as paprika, chilli flakes or fennel seeds. Over time, you may find you wish to change the basic palette of ground spices and seeds, so if you're not using cumin seeds with regularity then swap them for something else.

A Worthy Investment

When I left home to go to university my mother neatly packed in a spice tin as a final piece of treasure amongst my hand luggage. 'Don't forget this,' she said, 'it will be the one thing that stops you from being homesick.'

I chuckled all the way to my destination, thinking of how absurd her notion was. However never a truer word is spoken in jest. I still have the same spice tin to this day; I use it for my whole spices, and surely enough I packed my own daughter off to university last year! Yes, armed with a spice tin which made her the favourite girl in the house – 'The Chef'!

More specifically an Indian spice tin is called a masala dabba and I'll take an educated guess that almost every Indian household will have one. Either gifted in their trousseau (dowry) or presented upon leaving home for an independent life, like mine. It is usually a round stainless steel tin with seven compartments and usually comes with a small stainless steel teaspoon measure that fits in the tin.

A good masala dabba will have two lids: one that sits snugly on top of the seven round spice tins to prevent any cross contamination and loss of fragrance, as well as a second tightly fitting lid over the top to further seal out the air and light. You can then fill these compartments with your favourite and regularly used spices. A spice tin is much more than a handy way to store spices.

It maintains their quality, the essence, and shelf life. It also facilitates the cooking process, by making the spices easily available in a single movement, instead of the endless rummaging amongst glass bottles in the cupboard past their sell by date, whilst the food burns on the stove.

The most effective storage would be to have two spice tins, one containing the whole spices, which manages the early infusion process of a 'curry', and then the second tin containing the ground spices, which is the next process, post cooking the onions, tomatoes etc. This easy management of your spices will make the cooking process efficient and effortless. At a single stroke, you have streamlined the cooking process and become a pro. Welcome to real Indian cooking!

Discerning Spices

Today we almost take for granted the availability of such a wide range of spices but if you are discerning enough to cook for yourself then you'll want to achieve the best results you possibly can.

Great taste starts with high grade, pure essence, unadulterated spices, delicately harvested in their natural state; this will make a huge difference to the flavours you create. Spices should never be perfumed.

And like good coffee and whiskey you want to be very particular about the grade of spice and its provenance. Avoid using irradiated supermarket spices as they have been heat treated and will have lost their natural essential oils.

The emphasis should be on quality and purity; the flavour will be more concentrated and you will use less, making it more cost effective. The flavours will be punchier and shine through earlier, rather than dull and subdued. It is most important that spices do not contain additives as these will interfere with the pure essence of the spice and ultimately the flavour it yields.

Furthermore, it will affect the outcome of the dish and this is possibly where most people come unstuck and are hugely disappointed with the end result of their curry.

Preparing for Your Culinary Journey

In preparation for your journey through this cookery book I would recommend organizing some basic ingredients so that your daily cooking flows seamlessly and without stress.

Certain ingredients are present in almost every dish and so it is definitely worth preparing those ingredients in bulk to have in ready supply. Hot herbs such as garlic, ginger and chillies can be prepared and frozen ahead, so as to reduce the level of *mise en place* on every cooking occasion.

PREPARING GARLIC
You should start by peeling about 500g of garlic (watch my YouTube videos to get an idea of the process if you prefer), put the peeled cloves into a food processor, and add 1 tablespoon of rapeseed oil and a quarter teaspoon of salt.

Blitz the garlic until finely minced. Turn out into a plastic freezer storage bag. Flatten the mixture to the size of a thick sheet no more than 5mm; this will eliminate any air pockets and will enable you to break off pieces once it is frozen without the need to defrost it first.

Finely minced garlic will absorb into the cooking process easily, and so yield its flavours quickly into the dish.

Its easy absorption also means it is less likely to make your breath smell. You can repeat the same process with ginger and chillies; however, you can omit the oil for the ginger and chillies as they have a greater water content.

Youtube video.com/watch?v=AAs21c1t4ew
– Making garlic easy – Kumud Gandhi

How to Use & Store Fresh Coriander

Fresh coriander leaves are such a staple ingredient, both in the cooking process to release flavour and as a garnish at the end of a dish. I suppose it is the equivalent of what parsley is in Mediterranean cuisine. Once harvested, it has a notoriously short shelf life and can be a waste of money if not managed properly.

Here is a tip to get at least seven days' use from a bunch.

Start by gently bathing the coriander in a clean bowl of cold water. Soak and wash gently. Change the water at least once if necessary. Lift out of the water and shake off as much water as possible. Using a clean cloth, gently towel dry as much as possible. Spread the bunch over a clean tea towel, or something else that is absorbent so the coriander can drain effectively. Leave to dry at ambient temperature for 2-3 hours. The leaves should be mostly dry of moisture but still fresh and with just a little dampness to touch.

Now create a foil pouch by folding a large sheet of foil paper in half and fold down the two edges to create a bag, leaving it open at the top.

When the coriander is ready, place the coriander in the bag and refrigerate until you wish to use it. Since it's already washed that's one less job when you're cooking. If you've dried it correctly this technique should give you at least seven days' use.

Other herbs such as parsley, mint and sage can be prepared and stored in the same way to maintain freshness and shelf life.

In my recipes I talk about adding a 'three-finger pinch' of coriander.   Essentially, this equates to the equivalent of a tablespoon but if you've ever tried to pick up cut herbs with a tablespoon, you'll know it's quite difficult to do. So my 'three-finger pinch' is effectively using your thumb, index and middle finger to pick up a generous amount of fresh coriander.

Ghee

I am often asked about ghee and I find that I am usually trying to change a perception that ghee is bad for you.

Well if you look at the saturated fat content in isolation then I'm on a hiding to nothing – guilty as charged; it's high in fat. However, I never look at food in isolation, since it performs a biological reaction when it hits your body chemistry and this is where the benefit of ghee lies. I've grown up cooking with it, but always in the right context. Ghee is clarified or purified butter. It is lactose free and does not contain any milk solids as these have been removed in the boiling process.

Ghee therefore is composed of almost entirely saturated fat. OMG – if this is making you switch off already then I urge you to read on all the way to the bottom before you make a judgement.

In our cookery classes I talk about oils and virtues of one oil over another. The most important thing about cooking with oil is not to burn it or hydrogenate it. Using vegetable oils at too high temperatures can still achieve this, which means the oils become fat pockets in the body. Ghee is actually an ideal fat for frying because it has a high smoke point (where its molecules begin to break down) at 250°C (482°F), which is well above typical cooking temperatures of around 200°C (392°F) and above that of most vegetable oils.

This means ghee has a very stable saturated bond so it's less likely to form free radicals in the body (free radicals oxidize in the body to become bad cells and lock together to form clumps – which eventually can become a tumour or cancerous).

The research indicates that ghee is likely to reduce cholesterol both in the serum and intestine (really quite the opposite to the previous hype about ghee increasing cholesterol). It does so by increasing the stimulation of stomach acids – biliary lipids (the bile acid) to help the digestive process, whilst other fats, such as butter and oils, slow down the digestive process and can sit heavily in the stomach.

NUTRITIONAL BENEFITS & MEDICINAL PROPERTIES

When cooking lentils I always swap out oil with ghee to ensure maximum digestion of the lentils to prevent any gas and for the protein and mineral values to be absorbed more quickly.

Ghee is reputed to be good for nerves and the brain as it helps to rejuvenate body tissues, bones, hair and skin. It helps control eye pressure and is beneficial to glaucoma patients. I remember my mother always applying a light application of ghee 2-3 times a day for burns, blisters or grazes to the skin to speed up the healing process.

The Reasons to Season

In our classes at The Cooking Academy we explain the use of the spices in their flavour, character, and functionality.

We examine the chemical and medicinal context to enable students to understand the functional reasons for adding the spices to the recipe. Knowing the background of the ingredients also enables you to get the most out of the recipes from a nutritional and flavour perspective.

Therefore I have defined the herbs and spices by their flavours, characteristics and medicinal values so you can see their key attributes and this may help you to decipher particular ingredients you may wish to add in recipes to address certain health issues. If you see a symbol at the end of a particular recipe, I have included a quick reference symbol to help you identify the associated key health benefits.

- Ingredients that are good for the brain function
- Ingredients that are good for the heart and cardiovascular system
- Ingredients that are good for the immune system
- Ingredients that are good for the digestive system
- Ingredients that are good for wellbeing, skin and hair
- Ingredients that should be eaten in small doses

The Healing Properties of Spices

AJWAIN SEEDS

Ajwain is the seed of the thyme plant and is a member of the carrot and parsley family; it has a very distinct pungent flavour. Although ajwain is commonly referred to a seed, it is in fact a fruit pod, usually sautéed in oil or ghee in a tarka before adding vegetables or lentils. This tempering process does make the pungency dissipate a little. Ajwain is also used in breads and biscuits to counterbalance the effects of fried wheat, which can have an adverse effect on the stomach and cause flatulence.

Medicinally – Ajwain is a carminative ingredient and so is used in the treatment of indigestion. It also contain the highest levels of thymol which is a germicide containing antiseptic properties.

ALLSPICE

Contrary to popular belief, allspice is a plant in its own right. The round berries with a rough uneven texture are native to Jamaica. Allspice has a complex flavour tone; it is warm, pungent and fragrant and probably represents a combination of clove, cinnamon, nutmeg and pepper, hence the name. I love using allspice in baking, in fruity buns and Christmas cake, and like to pair it with ingredients such as rum and walnuts. Then for savoury food it's probably most used in my Caribbean and South American dishes. Commercially, allspice is commonly used in jerk seasoning, spice blends, spiced tea mixes, as well as certain types of curries, though usually these are non-Indian. Food producers use it in ketchup, pickles, and sausages. The flavour lends itself to robust ingredients such as beef, in meatloaf, pot roasts or burgers. Allspice would also be a good substitute for cloves.

Medicinally – Its properties are analgesic, antioxidant, aromatic, and a muscle relaxant. Like clove and nutmeg, it contains the essential oil eugenol that is a mild antimicrobial agent. When it's consumed, it helps suppress the growth of bad bacteria in the colon while encouraging the production of good digestive enzymes. Furthermore, studies suggest that allspice combined with garlic and oregano has an effect against E coli, salmonella and L. moncytogenes infection.

For centuries, the Mayan Indians used allspice to embalm the bodies of people of importance.

ASAFOETIDA

Is a resinous gum obtained from the roots of a herbaceous plant from the parsley family. As its name suggests, asafoetida has a fetid smell but as the dish cooks, the smell gracefully recedes and it delivers a smooth flavour reminiscent of leeks or celery. It is an umami food, a little bit like parmesan cheese or fish sauce where the smell is so off-putting that one would wonder why it was ever turned into an ingredient at all. However, the addition of this ingredient will accentuate the flavours in the dish and so it's worthy of adding for the deepening of the flavour alone, as well as the nutritional benefits.

Asafoetida complements most commonly used Indian vegetables such as potatoes, onions, cauliflower, peas, and quick-cooking greens. Whether making a more involved vegetable dish or a simpler stir-fry, you only need about ¼ teaspoon. Asafoetida should always be used with lentils and daal dishes to help the digestion and is usually added in the tarka along with mustard or cumin seeds, dried chillies, curry leaves, garlic and ginger.

Medicinally – Asafoetida is largely used as an antidote to flatulence caused by the fermentation of food in the gut. Fermentation may be caused by the delayed digestion of certain types of food such as beans, lentils, onions, garlic, oats, wheat and cruciferous vegetables. Asafoetida stimulates the mucous membranes in the lining of the alimentary tract in the body.

BAY LEAVES

This is a hugely underestimated spice in my opinion for something that yields so much flavour in the cooking process; however it takes a while for the flavours to release which is why it works well when cooked in soups, stocks and stews. Bay is a pungent spice with a sharp and bitter flavour; that said when cooked it has a warm aroma and is floral in taste with a very mild release of heat. Although bay is native to the Mediterranean, it is used extensively in Indian cooking with biriyani and other sauce-based dishes, and also as an ingredient in garam masala.

Medicinally – The chemical properties of bay make it a diuretic, helping to expel wastewater from the body. It contains antimicrobial properties that combat some of the most common pathogens, including Staphylococcus aureus. Furthermore, the oil extract or powdered bay leaf is effective in lowering blood glucose, cholesterol and triglyceride levels. Bay contains vitamin A, B and C, whilst the antioxidants are used as an antiseptic and digestive aid.

BLACK CARDAMOM

Black cardamom is much stronger than its green family member; it is bold and resinous with a smoky flavour. It is in fact smoke dried. The black cardamom is camphor-like in flavour. It is used with robust meats, such as chicken, lamb or beef in sauces. It is also an ingredient used to make garam masala.

Medicinally – Black cardamom is an antiseptic, antispasmodic, carminative, diuretic, and good for digestion. They are a good source of minerals like potassium, calcium, iron and magnesium.

BLACK PEPPER

It is historically the most commonly used spice in the world after salt, often referred to as 'The King of Spices'. Pepper gives heat and has a citrusy, yet sweet note with a camphor-like aroma.

Medicinally – The chemical in black pepper is piperine that makes it antimicrobial in nature. It is a natural antioxidant. It acts as an anti-inflammatory, and a remedy used to prevent the recurrence of illnesses such as fever, which is why it was so popular throughout Europe in the Middle Ages. It contains mainly vitamins A, C, E, K, niacin and beta-carotene; and traces of minerals such as iron, calcium and phosphorous. The amino acids contained by black pepper can enhance the absorption of other nutrients.

Black pepper is possibly the first organism to be used regularly as a food additive and preservative. Although salt proves a more effective preservative due to the ability to cure and dry out organic material, the antimicrobial potential of black pepper provides the chemical protection in preservation.

CHAAT MASALA

Chaat is the name for hot, tangy, sweet and umami flavours, and its masala is a blend of spices with such tones that together create a profusion of flavour in the dish. It is used in north Indian cuisine for street food dishes and like garam masala there is no one recipe for it. The flavour is characteristic of its salty and sour notes coming from the dried mango powder and the slightly strange sulphuric odour from the black salt (which is actually pink salt mined from the foot of the Himalayas). Those flavours are balanced by cumin, coriander, asafoetida, fennel and dried ginger. If you are buying a ready made chaat masala be sure to know its provenance: as with any spice blend the lower quality ones will become evident in the taste.

Medicinally – The properties of the ingredients have been covered in this chapter.

CHILLI

Yes, chillies are addictive! Capsaicin, the chemical contained in chillies, stimulates the brain to excrete endorphin and gives a sense of pleasure when eaten. Different varieties of chillies will produce different flavours; red chillies are sweeter since they have ripened, whilst the green chillies have a slightly bitter tone. If it's a hot chilli you may not be able to recognize the sweetness as the heat will pervade your senses. Scotch bonnet chillies are hot, sweet and slightly fruity in their flavour, which is why they tend to be used to make hot pepper sauces. Green finger chillies are most commonly used in Indian cooking; they have a light citrusy flavour whilst still packing a punch.

The heat of a chilli comes from the capsaicin, which sits on the inside of the chilli facing the core, and seeds. The seeds are not the hottest part of the chilli; there is simply transfer of heat from the capsaicin to the seeds over a period of time. If you want a milder chilli then look out for chillies with thicker flesh structures, as the capsaicin will have dispersed a little and reduced the heat level.

When using chilli powders look for the pure varieties rather than blended chilli powders since they are adulterated with other spices that will confuse the flavours of your dish. Invest in a good Kashmiri chilli powder too; this will give you intensity of colour and flavour but without the heat. A Madras chilli powder sits between the hot chilli variety and the Kashmiri chilli powder. Using milder chilli powders will give you depth of flavour, without overheating the dish. Chilli powders should be pure; never buy chilli that is a composite of a number of ingredients, as you will lose the essence of the spice.

Medicinally – A chilli a day will keep the doctor away, and here's why. Chillies are an excellent source of vitamin A, B, C and E, B6 and with minerals like magnesium, folic acid, potassium, thiamine, and copper. Chillies contain seven times more vitamin C than oranges.

The capsaicin in chillies contains beta-carotenoids, which are powerful antioxidants; these destroy harmful, potentially cancerous cells, which roam the body damaging other cells or nerve and blood vessels. The antioxidants help with conditions such as arthritis, like osteoarthritis and rheumatoid arthritis. They also dilate airways of the lungs, which reduces asthma and wheezing.

Chillies act as a detoxifying agent as they help to digest food and remove toxins whilst increasing the supply of nutrients to the tissues, thus helping to fight infections, and act as a natural antibiotic. Vitamin C, beta-carotene and folic acid are all minerals in chillies that reduce the risk of colon cancer.

CINNAMON

Cinnamon smells homely, exotic and Christmassy; it tastes warm and slightly bitter. But mostly, it's sweet, which is probably why our American friends put it in everything. It is a friendly spice that lives harmoniously with most ingredients and so works well with lamb and chicken, as well as nightshade vegetables such as butternut squash, tomatoes and capsicums. Cinnamon also enjoys the flavour of other sweet ingredients used in puddings and fruits; it particularly enhances the flavour of bananas, cherries, blueberries and apples. Cinnamon should be taken at the start of the day so conveniently is going to marry well with oats and cereals such as porridge.

In Indian cooking cinnamon bark is used to infuse the oil for robust ingredients such as lamb, chicken and aubergine dishes. Fennel seeds are frequently paired with cinnamon in vegetable dishes. Both the bark and powder are used regularly.

Medicinally – Cinnamon is a rich source of iron and calcium; it has the highest antioxidant strength of all the food sources in nature, many times more than is found in blueberries or apples. It is also a mild analgesic and an anti-inflammatory that can be used as an oil for aching joints common in arthritis. Cinnamon has inherent sweetness and is useful to curb your appetite since it can help to balance your blood sugar levels. It supports natural production of insulin to help stabilize blood sugar levels and so reduces the risk of type 2 diabetes. Cinnamon powder was traditionally used as a preservative. Aim to buy organic Sri Lankan cinnamon which is medicinally richer.

CLOVES

In taste, cloves are piquant, astringent, pungent and have a sweet fragrance. They have a warming effect, and as such are rarely used in the summer season in hot climates. Cloves pair well with rice, sauces, garam masala recipes, hot soups, teas, pickles as well as with apples, oranges, onions, ginger, chicken, lamb and pork. Cloves are also used in a powder form in preserves, drinks and puddings.

Medicinally – Cloves are rich in minerals such as calcium, iron, sodium, potassium, vitamin A and C; they also contain a chemical called 'eugenol' that inhibits the growth of bacteria, making them a natural antibiotic and germ killer. They also have antihistamine properties. Cloves are widely used in the commercial preparation of oral hygiene products such as toothpaste and mouthwash. Clove oil is a traditional remedy for toothache and I confess that it works for me too. I also use clove oil as an emollient on holiday as the eugenol chemical keeps the mosquitoes at bay.

CORIANDER

Coriander is both a herb and a spice, extensively used in many regions of the world. Such a versatile spice wears so many hats and yet is so unassuming in the spice tin. In Indian cookery, both the seed and the leaf are extensively used as a staple in most sauce bases and spice blends. As a raw seed, coriander has a musky floral aroma punctuated by a fresh, citrusy note. When roasted it has a nutty aromatic flavour, almost cardamom-like. Coriander is the bedrock of most Indian cuisine so it's important that the seeds are fresh, and ground regularly. Look out for plump coriander seeds with a greenish yellow hue; they are the most naturally fragrant and aromatic. Don't use brown seeds or brown ground coriander; it is a sign of age and irradiation. As they are so light they lose their colour quickly under stressful conditions.

Medicinally – Coriander in the leaf form can help to lower blood cholesterol as it is a diuretic, thus also stimulating the kidneys as it expels water from the body. Coriander leaf is very low in calories and contains no cholesterol. However, its deep-green leaves and stems possess good amounts of antioxidants, flavonoids, essential oils, vitamins, and dietary fibre, which help reduce bad cholesterol while raising good cholesterol levels. Its leaves and seeds contain many essential volatile oils. The herb is a good source of minerals like potassium, calcium, manganese, iron, and magnesium. It is also rich in many vital vitamins, including folic acid, riboflavin, niacin, vitamin A, beta-carotene, and vitamin C, which are essential for optimum health.

CUMIN

Cumin is widely popular across the globe for its distinctive strong aroma, and earthy flavours that leave a warm perception on the taste buds that comes from the essential oils in the seed. Its earthy tones make it a good flavour base and so it's a staple ingredient in condiments, sauces and most dishes whether it's a sauce or dry dish.

Medicinally – Cumin seeds contain numerous phytochemicals that are known to have antioxidant, carminative and anti-flatulent properties. The seeds are an excellent source of dietary fibre. The active ingredients in cumin help to mobilize the guts – so improve digestion. This spice is an excellent source of minerals like iron, copper, calcium, potassium, manganese, selenium, zinc and magnesium. Copper is required in the production of red blood cells. Cumin also contains very good amounts of B-complex vitamins such as thiamine, vitamin B6, niacin, riboflavin, and other vital antioxidant vitamins like vitamin E, vitamin A, and vitamin C.

CURRY LEAF

No, Curry leaves have nothing to do with curry powder! They are a staple ingredient of south Indian food but also used in most vegetarian dishes too in Gujarati cuisine. They are dark green shiny leaves with a wonderful aroma when infused with oil that gives a nutty yet citrusy flavour. They grow like hedgerows in India, by the roadside, two a penny. Curry leaves are added to the tarka, into the oil or ghee once the mustard seeds or chillies have infused and just before the main ingredient like daal or aubergine is added. I think curry leaves really lift the aroma in a dish as well as making the kitchen aromatic and luring hungry feasters to the dinner table.

Medicinally – Curry leaves contain properties that are antioxidant, antimicrobial, anti-inflammatory and anti-carcinogenic. The primary nutrients found in curry leaves are fibre, calcium, phosphorous, iron, magnesium, copper and minerals. It also contains various vitamins: vitamin C, vitamin A, vitamin B, vitamin E, as well as antioxidants, plant sterols, amino acids, glycosides and flavonoids. Like asafoetida, curry leaves assist with the digestion of food and over production of acid secretion in the stomach which can cause peptic ulcers.

DILL – THE SEED AND HERB PLANT

Dill is a member of the parsley family with a long history of use in medieval Europe. Both the seed and herb plant can be eaten. The dill seed has a similar look and smell to caraway seeds and is often mistaken for the same.

Indian dill, known as sowa, has a slightly longer and thinner seed. Dill seed has a camphor-like, slightly bitter yet delicate flavour; the seeds have a stronger flavour than the plant. The seeds should be used in breads and stews, and are particularly useful in pickling. When combined with vinegars, garlic, sugar, salt, and pepper, it produces that delightful puckery flavour of pickled cucumber and gherkins. Dill as a herb pairs very well with fish, chicken, omelettes or in potato salads. In Indian cookery the fresh plant is widely used as a form of spinach and cooked with other vegetables; it is available in ethnic stores in the UK.

Medicinally – Dill weed helps to relax the stomach muscles; by doing so it improves digestion, enabling the intestinal gas to dissipate. As it is a relaxant, drinking dill tea is a good relief for insomnia. In India, the seeds have historically been boiled to make a weak tea, given to babies to ease colic, encourage sleep, and stop hiccups, since it produces a lulling effect. Dill seed is an active ingredient in the commercial product gripe water, specifically as a remedy for colic in infants.

Dill seed is rich in calcium; one tablespoon contains as much as 100 milligrams more than in 80ml of milk. It is also high in fibre, iron, and magnesium.

FENNEL SEEDS AND BULB

Fennel is perhaps one of the most versatile herbs you can grow. Once established in the garden, it will provide a graceful backdrop for shorter herbs. Fennel foliage will attract the swallowtail butterfly caterpillars, which feed on the leaves. I love growing fennel for those reasons as much as eating it fresh from the garden, and picking the seeds in early September; they taste delicious in salads. I use fennel seeds in a number of spice blends, marinades and chutneys. It adds a fragrance to the dish which leaves the palate quite refreshed. You'll see it included in a number of recipes in this book.

As well as its culinary use fennel is a popular ingredient in many cosmetic preparations, including anti-wrinkle cream, perfume, and soap. If you are creative in cooking you'll find the liquorice-like flavour of fennel quite agreeable, which makes a tasty addition to spice blends, sauces, roasts, grilled fish, sausages, Chinese marinades, curries, and cheese.

All parts of the plant are edible, and the celery-like stalks of sweet fennel can be eaten as a vegetable, raw or cooked. Florence fennel has a bulbous base that can be roasted, or shredded into a coleslaw or salad. Note that a traditional Italian salad will include fennel to accompany the main course especially if it is a protein dish like lamb.

For me, it is its medicinal values that encourage my use of it in cooking, as well as the sweetness of flavour; it is a carminative therefore a brilliant digestive aid, used to help break down acid and to digest proteins, especially red meat. Fennel is also recommended as a detoxifier of the liver, to cure colic in infants, and to relieve congestion of the lungs, hence infants with colic are given fennel water and many cough preparations contain fennel.

The Latin word for fennel, foeniculum, meaning 'little hay', is thought to describe its sweet aroma, although it may be a reference to the fact that it was fed to goats to stimulate their milk production. This principle is also used in India for nursing mothers; dill is commonly interchanged with fennel to increase the mother's milk supply to her child. Dioscorides and Hippocrates believed fennel would stimulate milk production in nursing mothers. Dioscorides found fennel to contain diuretic properties, and recommended it for urinary tract disorders. Fennel was one of the four 'warming seeds' and declared by the Anglo-Saxons to be one of the nine sacred herbs that would cure the nine causes of medieval diseases.

Medicinally – Fennel seeds are very rich in fibre, vitamins and minerals including magnesium, calcium, folic acid, potassium, and iron, phosphorous and vitamin C. Fennel is very effective against digestive problems. In Indian homes, fennel seeds are routinely chewed after meals to aid digestion after a meal while also acting as a mouth freshener. These days fennel tea is often available for beneficial effects upon the stomach since it can bring relief to a bloated stomach, cramps, acid indigestion, and many other digestive tract maladies. Fennel is an active ingredient in commercial acid reflux remedies such as Gaviscon and gripe water.

FENUGREEK

This spice is highly revered in Indian cuisine, often referred to as methi both in the seed form as well as the leaf. The seeds are paired with bitter vegetables, such as okra and spinach, and used in the tarka process. Fenugreek is not the most aromatic of spices when cooking; it has a fairly pungent aroma, with a bitter taste, a little bit like burnt celery.

Medicinally – Fenugreek seeds are rich in minerals such as iron, potassium, calcium, selenium, copper, zinc, manganese and magnesium. In the vitamin department, it contains thiamine, folic acid, riboflavin, niacin, and vitamins A and C. It contains protein, fibre, potassium, iron and alkaloids.

Fenugreek is excellent at lowering LDL (bad) cholesterol levels by discouraging bile salts from absorbing into the colon, while at the same time binding to toxins so they can be escorted from the body. Furthermore the amino acids in the seeds help lower the rate of glucose absorption in the intestines, which lowers blood sugar levels in patients with diabetes.

GARLIC

I have yet to come across a country that doesn't use garlic to prepare food in some way. It is in my opinion a bit of a superstar. I love the flavour it brings to food; I know that I would struggle to cook without it. However, there are communities in India that forbid the use of garlic or an onion on religious grounds as it is considered an aphrodisiac and yet they manage to create very tasty vegetarian food!

Garlic is pungent and has heat properties. The process of roasting garlic mellows the pungency and releases the sugars in it, giving a caramelized taste. Garlic works beautifully when matched with chilli, onions, ginger, turmeric, greens, beans, spinach, chicken, pork and seafood. It is also the flavour of ingredients paired together such as ginger, onions, tomato, olives and chillies.

Garlic is best consumed in its raw state and there are interesting ways to enjoy it raw without it leaving an unpleasant taste, in dishes such as salsa verde, garlic dips made with mayonnaise or Greek yoghurt. Cooking garlic lightly is most practical, or adding it towards the end of the cooking process.

Medicinally – Garlic is another superfood, bringing plentiful health benefits, and so it certainly features widely in my recipes. Garlic is a potent antioxidant that has been found to inhibit the formation of cancerous cells, and is currently being studied by the National Cancer Institute. It may be effective in fighting stomach, skin and colon cancer.

Garlic has great value as a long-term dietary supplement, helping to maintain healthy circulation, balance blood sugar and pressure, reduce fat levels in the blood, and improve resistance to infection. It can be taken with conventional antibiotics to support their action and ward off side effects. Studies have shown that garlic provides protection against heart disease. The studies revealed that garlic decreases total serum cholesterol levels while increasing serum HDL cholesterol levels. HDL cholesterol, also known as 'good' cholesterol, is a protective factor against heart disease.

Garlic is also used in treating upper respiratory infections, late-onset diabetes, urinary infections, asthma, sinusitis, arthritis, and ulcers.

Its mineral contents include vitamin B6, vitamin C, manganese, calcium, copper, phosphorous, iron, and potassium.

In rare instances, garlic may cause gastrointestinal symptoms; in some people, the use of garlic may change the flora of the intestine, creating an allergic reaction.

GARAM MASALA
Garam masala literally translates into 'a warm blend of spices'; it is a key spice blend in the cupboard and is an absolute essential to north Indian cookery. A good garam masala is worth its weight in gold, so always grind your own or only purchase from a trusted source. It is usually added just before serving the dish to elevate its flavour, along with lemon juice and fresh coriander, though this can vary a little in practice from recipe to recipe. There is no single recipe for this spice blend; it varies from state to state and family to family. The core ingredients are usually the same, and comprise of cinnamon, cardamom – green and black, cloves, black pepper, star anise, nutmeg, mace and bay leaves. The heat in this spice blend is subtle and comes from a number of ingredients like cloves, cinnamon, and black pepper.

Chilli powder is not added since it is not designed to be hot, furthermore it should not contain cumin or coriander as these are important ingredients in their own right and are usually added to the recipe separately along with chilli and turmeric. Be aware of commercial recipes as they can often contain poor grades of spices and be imbalanced in flavour, usually in favour of the cheaper ingredients. As this spice is added at the end of the dish, if its properties are imbalanced then you will taste the disparate flavours and could end up ruining a good recipe.

Medicinally – Garam masala contains a number of key spices that have been addressed in this chapter.

GINGER
Ginger is among my favourite plant foods; it adds such warmth and radiance to a dish, an instant pick-me-up in food. It tastes sweet, a little spiky, and citrusy but, above all, warm and cleansing. It is one of the oldest herbs across the globe. There are sightings of ginger in recipes dating back to 1100 in England yet we have only really taken to ginger over the last 20 years in mainstream cooking. Though called a root, it is actually a rhizome and part of the turmeric and galangal family. It is used in the fresh form, as a dried powdered spice, as a pickle or as a dried fruit in baking and desserts. However, it is worth noting that dried ginger and fresh ginger have very different flavours and the two are not interchangeable. Dried ginger is much hotter, whereas fresh ginger has a mellow, full-bodied taste. Ginger is a very yielding plant; it sits comfortably with most ingredients such as casseroles, stir-fries, cakes, and even drinks: alcoholic or smoothies.

Traditionally, ginger was used as a preservative; in Greece, they wrapped it in bread for longevity, which is the origin of gingerbread.

Medicinally – Ginger is quite the superfood, wonderful for warming up the entire body and fighting off nasty germs. Its therapeutic actions are anti-nausea, digestive stimulant, circulatory stimulant, antibacterial and anti-inflammatory. It is used for its carminative properties in alleviating symptoms of gastrointestinal distress. It can also help to lower cholesterol levels and reduces the risk of heart disease and stroke.

Researchers at the highly respected journal, *The Lancet,* have demonstrated that ginger beats dimenhydrinate, the main ingredient in motion sickness drugs such as Dramamine, for controlling symptoms of seasickness and motion sickness.

GREEN CARDAMOM
Cardamom reminds me of vapour rub; it has distinct notes of camphor and eucalyptus. Its flavour tone sits in the citrus camp, though actually it is a member of the ginger family. The fresh and floral notes from the cardamom make it ideal for cutting through fattiness, especially with ingredients such as lamb, cream, nuts, rich coffee or buttery rice. Cardamom also pairs well with fruits such as apricots, mangoes, pears, bananas and coconut. When used with other spices, cardamom blends easily with cinnamon, coriander, saffron, and ginger.

Medicinally – Cardamom has antibacterial and antifungal properties. It plays an essential role in the stimulation of your digestive tract as well as helping to break down lactose. This is primarily the reason why cardamom is added to Indian tea – chai; as well as providing the aromatic taste, the cardamom helps to stimulate both the appetite as well as create gastric juices for the eventual breakdown of food. Cardamom can also be used as a preservative agent when the seeds are ground to a powder form.

JAGGERY

Jaggery (otherwise known as gor in Hindi) is a natural sweetener made by the concentration of sugar cane juice without the use of any chemicals, synthetic additives or preservatives. Jaggery is used to provide a sweet balancing agent in food, often used to cut out the over-acidic taste of tomatoes in a sauce, and provide a smoother finish to dishes with lemon juice. It acts as a balancing agent in food. If you are unable to find jaggery, try using honey or a little brown molasses sugar.

Jaggery is made by boiling the juice of the sugar cane to eliminate the water content, creating a rich concentrate of sugar, which is then dried and fully matured.

Medicinally it contains an enormous wealth of minerals, protein and vitamins, including iron and copper, which in the form of jaggery is far richer than white sugar. The magnesium content helps the muscles, nerves and blood vessels to relax and so it helps in relieving the symptoms of asthma, migraine, tension and soreness in muscles. It is also a very good source of manganese and selenium.

I highly recommend that white sugar is replaced with jaggery or brown molasses sugar wherever possible as sugar is highly processed and contains a cocktail of chemicals, sulphur dioxide, lime, phosphoric acid, formic acid and bleaching agents.

MANGO POWDER

Mango powder is one of those little hidden nuggets in the spice box, used in a number of spice blends such as chaat masala as well as individually. It is used to provide a distinct balance of citrus' sour or tart note with an underlying sweetness in a dish without the moisture that would come from using lime or lemon juice. Mango powder is made from green mangoes that have been dried and powdered and is called amchur (also spelled amchoor) in Hindi.

It works particularly well in stir-fries, vegetable dishes and chutneys. Mango powder has the same tenderizing qualities as lemon or lime juice making it a particularly good addition to marinades. You should add to your dish towards the end of cooking to retain its sweet and sour flavour.

Medicinally, mango powder has been linked to a range of benefits, many of which are associated with mangoes themselves. For example mango powder is thought to help improve digestion, partly because of the fibre that is present. Likewise, the antioxidants in mango powder could make it relevant for reducing disease risk, promoting skin health and improving overall wellbeing. This is supported by scientific research and one particular study found that a dose of 300mg per day was able to significantly improve multiple outcomes related to diabetes, including microcirculation and glucose metabolism, and a similar effect on blood sugar has also been found for freeze-dried mango.

MUSTARD SEEDS

Mustard seeds and their oils are used extensively in Indian cooking. They are pungent and bitter in their raw form; however, once heated the seeds will change flavour quickly, producing a sweetness that will uplift any pickles, preserves, stir-fries and curries. Black or brown seeds have a more intense flavour than the yellow ones. The aroma and pungency of mustard comes from the enzymes that convert into mustard oil once the seed is broken or popped, however this nasal burning bite is reduced when mixed with other liquids.

Unless you're using them in a pickle and adding to vinegar or brine, mustard seeds need to fry and pop in hot oil to release their full potential. In quick stir-fries, pop them in hot oil with asafoetida, and finely chopped ginger and garlic. They can burn quite quickly so have the other ingredients ready to add soon after the popping has subsided.

Medicinally, mustard is a member of the brassica family and both the seeds and its leaves are highly regarded as a medicinal powerhouse in Indian cuisine. They are very rich in phytonutrients, minerals, vitamins, antioxidants and essential oils. Its seeds are high in calories; 100g of seeds contain 508 calories. However, they are a good source of dietary fibre, and recommended in the management of cholesterol and weight reduction programmes. Mustard seeds contain flavonoid antioxidants such as carotenes, vitamin A, C and vitamin K. Calcium, manganese, copper, iron, selenium and zinc are some of the minerals especially concentrated in these seeds.

Mustard greens are used extensively in Indian cooking as they are an excellent source of essential B-complex vitamins such as folates, niacin, thiamine, riboflavin, pyridoxine (vitamin B6), and pantothenic acid. These vitamins are essential in the sense that the body requires them from external sources to replenish. These B-complex groups of vitamins help in enzyme synthesis, nervous system function and regulating body metabolism.

NUTMEG & MACE
This is a tale of two spices – they grow from the same fruit of the nutmeg tree. The nutmeg is the oval-shaped pit, which is the fruit; mace is the outer webbing that surrounds the nutmeg, which is bright red in colour when harvested. The mace is removed, dried and then ground into a coarse powder that turns an orange colour. The nutmeg is dried and left whole for grating on use.

Nutmeg has a nutty, sweet flavour. Its pungency makes it ideal for savoury and sweet dishes such as pies, cakes, soups, sausages and preserves. Both nutmeg and mace are used to make garam masala.

Nutmeg pairs well with a number of other spices such as cardamom, cinnamon, cloves, coriander, cumin, ginger, pepper, cranberries, thyme, and vanilla. You can use nutmeg in savoury dishes like asparagus, beans, cabbage, eggs, fish, lamb, onion, carrots, pumpkin, potatoes, sausage, as well as coffee drinks. Mace on the other hand is primarily used in desserts and rice dishes.

Medicinally – Nutmeg and its oil are used for illnesses related to the nervous and digestive systems. The compounds in this spice such as myristicin and elemicin have a soothing as well as stimulant effect on the brain. Nutmeg oil contains eugenol, which is used in dentistry for toothache relief. Furthermore, the oil is also used as a local massage to reduce muscular pain and rheumatic pain of the joints; it is an active ingredient in a number of topical anti-inflammatory products for muscle ache.

This spice is a good source of minerals like copper, potassium, calcium, manganese, iron, zinc, and magnesium. It is also rich in many vital B-complex vitamins, including vitamin C, folic acid, riboflavin, niacin, vitamin A and many flavonoid antioxidants like beta-carotene.

ONION SEEDS
Onion seeds are also known as nigella seeds.

Contrary to popular belief they are not from the onion family at all, but rather the *nigella sativa* plant. The black seeds taste like a combination of onions, black pepper, and oregano. They have a pungent, bitter taste and smell. The dry-roasted seeds are used in curries, vegetables, and pulses. I often use onion seeds when I am trying to cut out onions but want the flavour of onions.

Medicinally, onion seeds are antifungal and known to be resistant against a number of superbugs. They contain up to 38 percent oil and up to 2.5 percent essential oil. They also contain calcium, fibre, iron, potassium and sodium. Nutritionally, the seeds contain 21 percent protein, 35 percent carbohydrate and 36 percent fat.

PAPRIKA

Is potentially the darling of the spice cupboard for the newcomer to spices, allowing a little experimenting with flavours without the heat.

Paprika is a member of the chilli family, harvested from the capsicum to create pure paprika; it has a warm, rich fruity flavour and provides depth and gravitas to a dish. Hungarian, Spanish and Indian paprika are amongst the best varieties in the world. There are essentially three types of paprika; regular paprika has no heat but brings depth of flavour, and immense colour and vibrancy, and is the variety commonly used in Indian cookery. Sweet paprika is often labelled as Hungarian paprika and is distinct for its fruity flavour and intensity.

Spanish smoked paprika is cultivated from dried chillies that are smoked over oak giving the spice a woodsy, smoky flavour that is great for stews and roast meats. Since it is made from mild chillies and capsicum it isn't technically paprika but it sold as smoked paprika. Smoked paprika is rarely used in Indian cooking. Paprika and chilli flakes are natural bedfellows: the chilli flakes provide the speckled and slightly random heat whilst the paprika gives flavour.

Medicinally – Paprika comes loaded with carotenoids, the pigments that give it its beautiful deep colour. It also contains antioxidants, and a range of phytochemicals and antibacterial agents to lift the immune system. The vitamin A in paprika is excellent for the eyes, supporting night vision and healthy cell development. Just 1 tablespoon provides 100% of your RDA. Furthermore, paprika is rich in vitamin C, E, K, potassium, magnesium, phosphorous and iron.

SAFFRON

As the most expensive spice in the world, I am glad to say that a little saffron goes a long way. It is a very intense spice, with a complex taste that is bitter, semi-sweet, slightly metallic and sometimes synthetic. It works best when soaked for a few minutes; use the soaking water in the cooking process to harness all its flavour. Since it is such an intense spice, use with caution, as it can easily overpower a dish. In Indian food, saffron is used with rice recipes like biriyani and sweet dishes such as halvas, gulab jamons, kulfi and milk puddings. Saffron is harvested from the stamen of a crocus flower; it should be coarse in texture, like horsehair, so if it is soft it could be of a poor grade.

Medicinally – Saffron is a good source of minerals such as copper, potassium, calcium, manganese, iron, selenium, zinc and magnesium, as well as antioxidants and carotenoids. Additionally, it is also rich in many vital vitamins, including vitamin A, folic acid, riboflavin, niacin, and vitamin C.

STAR ANISE

This spice is a popular flavour for alcoholic drinks such as ouzo, raki, and sambuca. Star anise contains the flavour compound anethol that gives a sweet and liquorice flavour. It has similar flavour notes to fennel, anise seeds and tarragon. Star anise is used widely with duck and pork dishes, as well as apples or mulled wine. Its autumnal cinnamon-like sweetness pairs well with fruits, sauces and desserts. Star anise is used to make garam masala and Chinese five spice.

Medicinally – Star anise contains properties that are antibacterial, antioxidants, and antifungal. It also contains antiviral properties that are contained in medication that is marketed as Tamiflu. The seeds are an excellent source of many essential B-complex vitamins, A and C, calcium, iron, copper, potassium, manganese, zinc and magnesium.

TURMERIC

This spice has to be the most hidden jewel in the spice cupboard of all time! Commonly known to most as the yellow food colouring in Indian recipes, that stains your clothes, this little gem is actually a superpower of the spice grail.

Turmeric is a staple in most dishes in Indian food. It is a member of the rhizome family, a root, along with ginger and galangal. Turmeric has an amazing yellow golden hue, which is the source of its powerful beta-carotene properties. Fresh turmeric is eaten as a pickle and grated, into stir-fries, instead of using the dried powder. Turmeric is slightly bitter in taste but has an orangey ginger flavour and earthy tone. Turmeric was traditionally used as a preservative for food.

Medicinally – Turmeric has had a long-standing ovation in Asia for its many medicinal values; it contains an active phytochemical compound, known as 'curcumin'. This compound has been extensively researched and found to have such powerful medicinal values and is an extremely potent antioxidant. However, traditionally known for its anti-inflammatory effects, turmeric also has antibacterial and digestive properties, killing yeasts and parasites internally in the gut. These are some of the more simple values; its real benefits lie in the effect on the brain. Curcumin breaks up heavy metals and the hard protein plaques that are found in the brains of Alzheimer's patients. Clinical trials are currently underway concerning this benefit. Studies show that the curcumin-treated patient group also had less blood vessel growth in fat tissue. Blood glucose, triglyceride, fatty acid, cholesterol and liver fat levels were also lower.

The bottom line is that turmeric is a powerhouse of goodness and should be incorporated into your diet at every opportunity.

Indian Breakfasts

I am frequently asked 'What's a typical Indian breakfast?' The answer is not so straightforward since I'm not actually sure there is one. Of course Indians do eat breakfast which usually tends to be any kind of 'snack' and the choices will vary from family to family and region to region. Since India itself is so diverse, there is no common Indian breakfast as typical as bacon and eggs.

I think the expression that is most commonly used is 'naashta', and it denotes interim food, 'snacky' food. I suppose the reality is that you could eat the same kind of food at any time of the day as a snack.

If I were to think of a good Indian breakfast, it would typically be made from local and seasonal ingredients, perhaps containing speciality ingredients of the local area, so I'm thinking dosa and vada in the south and typically stuffed parathas in the north or dishes such as handvo and dhokla if you're from the western region in Gujarat.

Breakfast is always vegetarian, in keeping with the Hindu principle of vegetarianism; it is usually warm, designed to kick-start the metabolism.

Tea, however, is probably the common binding factor throughout all of India, peppered with a little ginger or cardamom depending on your geography (you can find a couple of tea recipes in the drinks chapter).

Here is a selection of some of my favourite dishes, recipes that I have grown up with that would be a tasty start to the day.

Anda Bhurji – Spicy Scrambled Eggs

Of course I love my plain scrambled eggs with a bit of salt and pepper but sometimes it's nice to have a bit of spice in the mornings and embellish the humble scrambled eggs. It also makes the eggs go further with the use of the usual fridge or store cupboard ingredients such as onions and tomatoes. Although this recipe is in the breakfast section I'm just as likely to eat this for lunch or supper.

Serves 4

Ingredients:
2 tbsp. oil
1 small onion, finely diced
30g broken cashew nuts
2 medium tomatoes, juice drained, finely chopped
¼ tsp finely chopped green chillies
1 tsp garlic – finely chopped
1 tsp ginger – finely chopped
¼ tsp turmeric
¼ tsp salt
6 eggs whisked lightly
Pinch of salt
Pinch of hot chilli powder
3-finger pinch of fresh coriander
Finely chopped chives to garnish

1. Heat the oil gently in a pan, add the onions and cashew nuts, stir and cook for 2-3 minutes until softened on a low heat so as not to brown the onions.

2. Increase the heat temporarily, add the drained tomatoes and stir through; once it starts to sizzle again, lower the temperature back to low to maintain cooking on a gentle heat, until the tomatoes are soft. This should take a minute or two.

3. Now add the green chillies, garlic and ginger, stir well until the spices release their aroma, then add the turmeric and salt. Stir well to incorporate all the spices and cook for a minute or until the oil separates from the mixture.

4. Meanwhile crack the eggs into a bowl and whisk, adding a pinch of salt and chilli powder. Add the whisked eggs to the pan. Increase the heat to high. Vigorously stir the egg mixture around and break the bigger clumps up. Add the chopped coriander and stir to incorporate all the flavours.

5. Turn the heat off, sprinkle with the chopped chives and serve immediately with a chapatti or paratha.

Batata Poha – Flaked Rice with Lightly Spiced Potato

This is a regular dish in my family home and that of my siblings, whether it is served at breakfast or as an indulgent snack at tea-time. The name translates into batata – potato, and poha is flattened rice commonly eaten in Gujarat and Maharashtra.

Serves 4

Ingredients:
300g potatoes (raw)
100g beaten rice or poha
¼ tsp salt + ¼ tsp
1 tsp sugar
¼ tsp turmeric + 1 pinch
½ lemon – juice of, or 1 tbsp. if using bottled
2 tbsp. oil
1 tsp mustard seeds
¼ tsp asafoetida
10 curry leaves
¼ tsp finely chopped hot green chillies
3 tbsp. red skinned peanuts – roasted and lightly crushed
Fresh coriander – finely chopped
Fresh pomegranate seeds and coriander to garnish, more lemon juice if preferred

1. Boil the potatoes whole in a large pan with salted water until cooked but still firm. When cool enough to handle, peel the potatoes and cut into 1cm cubes. Set aside.

2. Wash the poha in a bowl of cold water, just as you would rice; rinse with a few water changes until the water runs clear. Strain the excess water from the poha in a sieve, without squeezing it. Leave the poha straining for 5 minutes then turn it out into a bowl.

3. Gently fold the ¼ tsp salt, sugar, ¼ tsp turmeric and the lemon juice into the poha by hand, ensuring you don't break the poha by overhandling, and set aside.

4. In a wide-based pan with a lid add the oil, and when the oil is hot add the mustard seeds. Sauté until they finish popping then add the asafoetida followed by the curry leaves and then the cubed potatoes and the green chillies, the pinch of turmeric and another ¼ tsp salt. Stir the ingredients, gently incorporating the spices into each other. Cook for 2-3 minutes.

5. Now add the peanuts and the drained poha and gently fold together. Place the lid on the pan and cook for 5 minutes on a very low heat to ensure that everything is cooked through and the flavours infuse without drying out.

6. When ready, remove from the heat, garnish with fresh coriander and finely chopped pomegranate seeds and a squeeze more lemon juice if required. Serve with a cup of tea.

Egg Roll Paneer Wrap

This dish could very easily be underestimated as a 'veggie wrap' but this is no ordinary wrap. It's born out of leftovers and makes a great breakfast, brunch or snack. Chapattis are often recycled into some other yummy dish and one of my favourites is eggy chapattis, I suppose a take on eggy bread. Throw into the mix some leftover paneer stir-fry and there you have it.

Makes 5 wraps

Ingredients:

For the batter:
5 tbsp. (about 60g) gram flour
½ tsp salt
1 tsp chilli powder
½ tsp turmeric
2 tbsp. fresh coriander – finely chopped
2 medium eggs – beaten
1 tbsp. cold water

For the filling:
3 tbsp. oil
1 tsp cumin seeds
1 inch stem of ginger – sliced into matchsticks – julienne
¼ tsp finely chopped green chilli
1 red onion – finely sliced
1 carrot – sliced into matchsticks – julienne
100g red or white cabbage – thinly sliced into julienne
150g paneer – cut into thin strips
1 tsp chilli powder
1 tsp turmeric
1 tsp ground roasted cumin
1 tsp salt
¼ tsp garam masala
1 tbsp. lemon juice
4 tbsp. fresh coriander roughly chopped
1 red pepper cut into thin strips

For the wraps:
5 chapattis or tortilla wraps – preferably wholemeal

Sweet chilli or sriracha sauce as a dressing if preferred

1. Make the batter by placing the gram flour, salt, chilli powder, turmeric and fresh coriander in a bowl; add the beaten eggs and 1 tablespoon of cold water, and whisk the ingredients together. The batter should be runny but thick enough to coat the chapatti. Set aside.

2. Now prepare all the vegetables for the filling and set aside.

3. Using a wide-based frying pan or wok, heat the oil and sizzle the cumin seeds, add the ginger, chilli and onion, and stir-fry and cook on a medium heat for 2-3 minutes until the onion softens a little.

4. Now add the carrot, cabbage and paneer followed by the chilli powder, turmeric, cumin powder, salt, garam masala, lemon juice and 1 tablespoon of the fresh coriander. Stir-fry, ensuring all the spices are thoroughly mixed together and beginning to release their flavour; you may need to moderate the temperature to ensure that all the moisture has evaporated.

5. Now add the red pepper and stir once more. When all the paneer is beginning to get crispy at the edges remove from the heat. Garnish with the remaining fresh coriander. Keep in a warm place. Now prepare the wraps by dipping the chapatti into the batter mixture.

6. Heat ½ tablespoon of oil in a frying pan wide enough to take the chapatti, place the batter-coated chapatti in the oil and coat for a minute or two on each side until the egg is cooked and the colour is light brown. Remove from the pan and place on some absorbent kitchen paper, and continue with the rest of the chapattis, adding oil as you need it.

7. When ready to assemble, place some of the stir-fry filling on the centre of the chapatti like a fajita, add a drizzle of sweet chilli or sriracha, and roll the chapatti very tightly. Cut on a diagonal in the middle and serve with a side salad or with a dip of your choice. Enjoy!

Spicy Breakfast Puri

Served with a generous mug of Darjeeling or of course the usual English breakfast tea, I can't think of a more indulgent Sunday morning feast, with the bonus of the leftover puris to snack on throughout the day. The slightly biscuity texture of the puris with the addition of the semolina flour makes them a great bready snack to take on long journeys too.

Serves 4

Ingredients:
200g wholemeal chapatti flour
30g semolina flour
2 tbsp. ghee
1 tsp bishop's weed seed – ajwain seeds
½ tsp asafoetida
2 tsp sesame seeds
1 tsp salt
½ tsp green or red chillies or to taste
½ tsp turmeric
½ tsp sugar
100ml hot water or until the dough has come together
Oil for frying

Equipment:
Thin rolling pin
Round rolling board
Oil vessel for frying puri (karahi)

1. Combine the two flours together; add the ghee and the bishop's weed seeds, asafoetida, sesame seeds, salt, chillies, turmeric and sugar. Rub the flour and spices together.

2. Add the water 1 tablespoon at a time and bring together into the dough as quickly as possible. Take a splash of oil onto your hands and then rub and knead to create a smooth dough.

3. Cover the dough in cling film and leave to rest in a warm place for 20 minutes.

4. Divide the dough into balls the size of a walnut.

5. Using a thin rolling pin, roll the dough balls out to a small saucer shape, approximately 2 inches in diameter, and 3mm thick, and rest on greaseproof paper whilst you roll out the remaining dough balls.

6. Heat the oil in a karahi and when the oil is hot enough fry the puri 2 or 3 at a time. Using a slotted metal spoon, remove from the oil when medium/suntan brown and place onto absorbent papers to drain.

Chef's Tip:

Remove the puris from the oil when they are light/medium brown as they will continue to cook and brown even after removed.

Paneer Burji

Homemade paneer has the look and texture of buffalo mozzarella and can be very crumbly in texture unlike the paneer blocks found in the supermarkets. Paneer is often perceived as being rather bland in itself; however it is a marvellous carrier for flavour, very much like tofu. This dish is really all about the delicious assortment of spices cooked with the onions, tomatoes and spinach, which the paneer readily soaks up hungrily.

Serves 4

Ingredients:
2 tbsp. oil
1 tsp cumin seeds
1 medium onion – thinly sliced
2 heaped tsp finely chopped garlic
1 tsp finely chopped ginger
½ tsp hot chilli powder
½ tsp salt
½ tsp ground coriander
½ tsp ground cumin
Pinch of turmeric
Small pinch of fresh coriander
60g spinach
50g garden peas
180g homemade paneer or if shop bought then grated paneer
1 medium tomato – diced
3-finger pinch of fresh coriander to garnish
Squeeze of fresh lemon
¼ tsp garam masala

1. Heat the oil in a frying pan, add the cumin seeds and sizzle for a few seconds before adding the sliced onion. Cook until lightly golden brown.

2. Now add the garlic and ginger and cook for two minutes on a low heat before adding the chilli powder, salt, ground coriander, ground cumin, turmeric and a small pinch of fresh coriander. Allow the spices to cook out for a few minutes to meld the flavour into the garlic and onions, before adding the spinach and peas.

3. Crumble in the fresh paneer, and stir and cook for 2 minutes before adding the fresh chopped tomato.

4. Add a little water if necessary to prevent the mixture from sticking and then garnish with fresh coriander; squeeze in the lemon juice and add the garam masala. You could also add thinly sliced spring onions as an option.

5. Serve with crispy roti or parathas and enjoy.

Street Food, Snacks & Starters

My own love of street food began as a child during visits to India. I remember walking through the markets surrounded by tempting aromas and readily agreeing when my cousin suggested buying a 'snack' or two. Even though we knew a feast would be waiting for us at home we became very skilled at feigning hunger to avoid disappointing my nannee (grandmother). It may not have been great for the waistline but it was certainly good for the soul and we always kept our little detours well hidden!

Like most things in India, the origins of snacks and quick food lie in its culture. Hospitality counts for a lot in Indian culture, and any good host should be able to whip up a snack at a moment's notice. There is even a saying drawn from an ancient scripture in Sanskrit: 'atithi devo bhavah' meaning 'consider the guest as God'.

Welcoming a guest into your home and not offering them some kind of snack or meal with a drink is considered the ultimate social faux pas and that is why the recipes in this chapter are absolute staples in many Indian homes. My father instilled this duty in me as a child and I would still find it alien not to offer guests to our home something to eat, even if their arrival was unannounced.

Here in Britain, we might react with something close to horror if a friend or relative turned up on our doorstep without so much as a text to warn us, but in India there is always a reason to entertain at any time of day, partly because there are so many more religious and cultural festivals throughout the year. What's more, you never think about portion size; you should be ready at a moment's notice, with plenty to go around just in case there is an extra mouth to feed.

What I like about street food is that it's real home cooked food brought out into the streets which means it's authentic and speaks of the real culture of the country, unlike the kind of Indian food you'll find in your typical local tandoori restaurant, which was originally created for a Western audience. Technically speaking, any food can be street food; it's the excitement and bustle of the roadside that gives it a sudden cachet.

Food has made a 360 degree turn; what started off as home recipes brought into the streets have now found their way back into the home as popular recipes to re-create the street version. Morning, noon and night, people queue at roadside cafes and stalls to fill up on tasty 'bitings' as they are often called, in places like Chowpatti in Mumbai.

No matter how overwhelmed with customers, the speed at which they churn out order after order, quite unflustered, is really a remarkable sight. Ingredients like whole wheat, lentils and rice can form the basis of dozens of different creations, used with other essentials including semolina flour, chickpeas, onions and potatoes. Armed with these key ingredients and the right spices, you can create something delicious in less than 15 minutes flat.

Here in the UK, we have just embraced this street food culture. Although we have been partial to our samosas and onion bhajias we're now beginning to see the real extent of street food, with dishes like papri chaat and pani puri, and it will change the way we eat forever. Most of all, I hope you take away from this chapter that convenience food need not be unhealthy, tasteless or expensive.

There is so much more to snacking than reaching for the nearest packet of crisps or biscuits. Therefore, it will take a little bit of forward thinking and practice, but you will never look back once you have sampled the tasty treats in store over the next few pages…

Parsi Style Fried Chicken

Parsi food combines both Persian and Gujarati influences. The people of Persia are famously fantastic cooks and have made a significant contribution to Indian food over the centuries. Our immediate neighbours in my ancestral home in India were Parsi and my early memories of their food were divine: so much theatre and such variety I always thought they were celebrating something since I couldn't imagine people eating so well on a daily basis!

Serves 4

Ingredients:
750g chicken thigh meat, wings or drumsticks – skin removed

For the marinade:
2 tbsp. lemon juice
1 tbsp. finely chopped garlic
1 tbsp. finely chopped ginger
1 tsp red chilli powder or black pepper
1 tsp ground cumin
1 tsp salt

For the coating:
100g breadcrumbs
Salt to taste
½ tsp freshly ground white pepper
A pinch of red chilli powder

4 medium eggs for the egg wash (after coating with breadcrumbs)

To deep-fry:
Oil for frying

1. Start with the marinade for the chicken. Place all the ingredients for the marinade in a non-metallic bowl. Stir well, taste and season.

2. Add the chicken, coat thoroughly and cover with an airtight lid. Place in the fridge overnight. Take the chicken out of the refrigerator an hour before you intend to use it.

3. When you are ready to fry the chicken, prepare the breadcrumb coating. Place the breadcrumbs, salt, white pepper and chilli powder onto a plate and mix well, then (now the unusual bit) roll each piece of chicken in the breadcrumbs to coat, pressing firmly, and set aside until you've coated all the pieces.

4. Heat the oil in a karahi on medium heat. Do not be tempted to raise the temperature. You do not want the oil to be too hot as this will cause the chicken to burn on the outside and remain raw on the inside.

5. Crack the eggs into a bowl and whisk until smooth. Season with salt and coarsely ground black pepper. Whisk again to mix well.

6. When the oil is ready dip each piece of chicken in the whisked egg mixture and gently drop into the hot oil. Fry a few at a time.

7. Use a slotted spoon to turn the chicken pieces occasionally. The chicken is done when it turns golden on the outside. Use a slotted spoon to remove from the oil and drain on paper towels.

Serving Tip:

Serve with a tamarind or chilli sauce.

Aloo Tikki

Aloo tikki are a potato-based snack. The word 'aloo' means potato and 'tikki' means small cutlet or croquette. It is a lightning-quick dish, eaten as street food or a late afternoon snack and can be easily turned into another Indian favourite, aloo vada. If you are making this dish for a dinner party or family meal, you can cook up some aloo tikkas as a starter or side dish. This recipe is versatile, so feel free to experiment with other ingredients like kidney beans or adding cooked chickpeas.

Serves 4

Ingredients:
200g King Edward or Maris Piper potatoes, peeled and quartered

1 tsp salt or to taste, added whilst the potatoes are boiling

1 tsp roasted cumin seeds

1 tsp turmeric

1 tsp finely chopped ginger

1 tsp green chilli, finely chopped

1 tbsp. lemon juice

A generous handful of chopped, fresh coriander

30g garden peas (optional)

2 strands spring onions, finely chopped

2 tsp toasted sesame seeds

5 tbsp. panko or normal breadcrumbs to coat before frying

2 eggs, beaten for egg wash

Oil to fry

1 tsp chaat masala (optional)

1. Boil the potatoes in salted water until cooked, drain. When cooled enough to handle, peel and grate (do not mash as the texture becomes too sloppy) then place in a bowl.

2. Add the cumin seeds, turmeric, ginger, fresh chilli, lemon juice, fresh coriander, peas, spring onions and toasted sesame seeds, mix well and season to taste.

3. Divide the filling into equal sized portions and shape into cookie-sized discs, around 4cm diameters by 1cm thick.

4. Place the breadcrumbs on a plate.

5. Egg wash the aloo tikki and then press them into the breadcrumbs, thoroughly coating them.

6. Place them on a tray in the fridge for about 30 minutes to set and firm up.

7. When you're ready to cook them, heat a few tablespoons of oil in a non-stick pan and when the oil is warm place them in. Fry on a medium heat for about 5-8 minutes on each side until they are crisp and golden. Add a little more oil to cook on the second side if required.

8. Serve with a chilli and mango dressing or hot and spicy tomato chutney and sprinkle with a little chaat masala if required.

Chef's Tip:
You could simply brush these with a little oil and roast them in the oven.
Even shallow frying requires very little oil – just 1 teaspoon per tikki.

Hakka Style Chilli Paneer

My hakka style chilli paneer is a firm favourite with my family and a great dish when you don't want a full meal. It is perfect as a starter for a dinner party or served as bowl food in mini portion sizes.

A few extra tips for you: serve the chilli paneer piping hot since cooked cheese can become a little chewy on cooling. In addition, if you wanted to convert this dish into a main course, add a little water towards the end of the cooking process and serve with noodles. For a vegan alternative just replace the paneer with tofu.

Finally, be careful with the batter consistency, as you don't want it as thick as you would for coating bhajias or tempura but not too thin otherwise it won't stick to the paneer pieces.

Serves 4

For the batter:
3 tbsp. plain flour
2 tbsp. cornflour
¼ tsp ground white pepper powder
1 tsp garlic, finely minced
Salt to taste
Approximately 100ml water – go by consistency not volume
2 tbsp. of plain flour for dusting the paneer
500ml rapeseed oil to deep fry paneer cubes

250g soft fresh paneer (firm Indian cottage cheese), cut into 1cm cubes
Flour for rolling the paneer in
2 tsp ginger, finely chopped
2 tsp garlic, finely chopped
2 stalks of celery, very finely chopped (like finely chopped onion)
2 green (or red) chillies, finely chopped
1 medium red onion, cut into 1cm cubes
2 medium capsicums, red and green for good colour, cut into ½ inch cubes
2 tbsp. soya sauce (or tamarind sauce can also be used)
3 tbsp. tomato ketchup
1 tbsp. hot red chilli sauce

2 tbsp. plain flour to dust
Oil to deep-fry

To garnish:
2 spring onions (green tops only)
Freshly chopped coriander

1. Heat 500ml of oil in a karahi.

2. Meanwhile prepare the batter to coat and fry the paneer by mixing the plain and corn flours together, then add the white pepper, garlic and salt and slowly add the water, using a whisk to avoid lumps.

3. Dust/roll the paneer pieces in the extra flour so that it absorbs any moisture.

4. Dip the paneer cubes in the batter and one by one place them into the hot oil. Deep-fry until they are a light golden colour. Don't fry too many at once otherwise they'll stick. When ready, remove from the pan and drain the paneer pieces onto some absorbent kitchen paper and set aside.

5. Use 2 tablespoons of oil from the karahi and place into a deep wok, add the finely chopped ginger, garlic, celery and chillies and fry until lightly golden (it should take about 4-5 minutes).

6. Add the onion and diced capsicum (bell pepper) pieces and fry on a medium heat for 2-3 minutes until they are just beginning to soften but retain their bite.

7. Reduce the heat and add the soya sauce, tomato ketchup and red chilli sauce. Stir well until the sauces have thickened and are sizzling hot.

8. Add the fried paneer pieces and increase the heat and stir-fry for 1-2 minutes until they become piping hot.

9. Remove from the heat and garnish with the green tops of spring onions and fresh coriander.

Chilli & Fennel Chicken Kebabs

For those of you who have attended my one day Indian class you'll know that this is an old favourite, and for something that is such low maintenance, it yields incredible flavour and is how a chicken kebab should really taste. Use this recipe for an easy BBQ chicken dish and you'll never be short of guests for sure.

Serves 4

Ingredients:
400g chicken thighs – each thigh deboned and cut into 4 pieces

For the spice blend:
2 tbsp. oil
2 tbsp. lemon juice
2 tsp finely chopped garlic
2 tsp finely grated/chopped fresh ginger
1 tsp ground cumin
1 tsp ground coriander
½ tsp dried chilli flakes
¼ tsp salt
1 tsp whole fennel seeds
1 tsp paprika
Large pinch fresh coriander

Trim the excess fat off the thighs and cut into 4 pieces or 2 inch cubes. Set aside. Place all of the ingredients for the spice blend into a bowl, mix well and taste. Add the chicken and set aside to marinate for at least 1 hour or up to 48 hours. Pan fry on a very low heat for 12 minutes, turning once after 7-8 minutes or place on a baking tray in the oven at 180°C for 20 minutes.

Urid Daal Bhajia

This dish is quite typical of both Gujarati and south Indian snacks: simple lentils soaked then ground to a thick paste, abundantly seasoned and then fried. In south India these bhajia are likely to be called 'vada' whilst in the north 'pakodas'. Although the pre-soaking of the lentils and then addition of yoghurt as a rising agent means a little planning ahead, the flavour is definitely worth the time. They are cost effective, tasty and a great use of lentils.

Makes approx. 30

Ingredients:

200g urid daal (lentils) soaked for 24 hrs then blitzed in a food processor

200g plain yoghurt

1½ tsp salt or to taste (salt will reduce in the frying process)

1½ tsp finely chopped green chillies

3 tsp freshly chopped ginger

2 tsp freshly chopped garlic

1 tbsp. lemon juice

2 tsp roasted cumin seeds

2 tsp ground cumin

1 large handful freshly chopped coriander

1 tsp toasted sesame seeds (optional)

1 tsp bicarbonate of soda

½ tsp baking powder

2 sprigs of spring onions – finely chopped, or 2 shallots finely chopped

Oil to fry – in a karahi

1. Wash the daal in warm water and soak overnight. The following day rinse out the water several times, drain and place into a food processor or use a hand blender and blitz with the yoghurt to a smooth texture. Turn out into a bowl.

2. Add the salt, chilli, ginger, garlic, lemon juice, cumin seeds, cumin powder, fresh coriander and sesame seeds (if using) and if at all possible rest overnight in the fridge. This will allow the yoghurt to soak into the lentil paste and make the bhajias very light, fluffy and digestible in texture. However, if you don't have time to soak the yoghurt then add the bicarbonate of soda and baking powder as a substitute. If you have soaked the batter overnight then remove from the fridge at least an hour before you're going to fry the bhajias and at this point add the spring onions or shallots, season once again to taste as the flavours will have changed since adding the onions or soaking overnight, and mix well.

3. Heat the oil in the karahi, take a tablespoon size of the mixture and gently drop it into the oil, and repeat with the rest of the mixture. Cook until golden brown and remove with a slotted spoon onto absorbent paper for a few minutes before serving.

Chef's Tips:

1. *This batter mixture can be frozen should you make excess.*

2. *Rest the bhajias after cooking as this will allow them to continue cooking through to the centre.*

3. *Serve with a tamarind and date dressing and generous dollops of natural yoghurt (this variation on the dish is known as dahi wadas).*

Aloo Chaat – Savoury Potatoes with Mustard Seeds

This savoury potato dish is a firm favourite in my house. Incredibly moreish and a doddle to make, no picnic in the park would be complete without a sizeable serving of this. Aloo chaat is very popular in most regions of India too, often as a street food served with puri (flatbreads) or as a rewarding snack during a long journey.

Aloo chaat can be eaten warm or at ambient temperature. However, cooled potatoes can be difficult to digest and can cause indigestion so the use of mustard seeds and asafoetida is important to make this dish easy on the stomach.

Serves 4-6

Ingredients:
450g potatoes, such as Charlottes or Jersey Royals when in season
2 tbsp. oil
1 tsp brown mustard seeds
1 tsp cumin seeds
¼ tsp asafoetida
1 small onion, finely chopped
½ tsp salt or to taste
½ tsp ground turmeric
½ green finger chilli, finely chopped
Juice of half a lemon
Handful of fresh coriander leaves – chopped

1. Boil the potatoes whole in a large pot of salted water until cooked, but still firm when the point of a knife is inserted. Drain and when cool enough to handle, peel or scrape and cut the potatoes into ½ inch (1cm) cubes. Set aside.

2. Heat the oil in a heavy pan over a medium-high heat. Add the mustard seeds and fry for 30 seconds or so until the mustard seeds start to pop. When they've finished popping add the cumin seeds and sizzle for just a second or two before adding the asafoetida.

3. Add the onion and cook for a few minutes until they are just softening and beginning to turn golden, and then add the salt, turmeric and green chilli as well as the potatoes. Stir the ingredients together to combine the spices into the potatoes and onions, and then reduce the heat.

4. Cook for a couple of minutes until hot and all the flavours have combined. Add the lemon juice and finish with a garnish of chopped coriander leaves.

5. Taste to adjust the seasoning accordingly and if the heat level is fairly mild you could add red chilli flakes to garnish. Serve immediately.

Chef's Tip:
You could add roughly ground red skinned peanuts as a garnish to add a little texture and protein to the dish.

Onion Bhajia

If you think you know onion bhajia, think again. I assure you these are nothing like the ones you may have tried in your local restaurant. My onion bhajia are much crispier and much more flavoursome.

To make sure your bhajia are the best in show, follow these tips. Don't allow them to get too brown in the oil, as they will continue to cook and brown after being removed from the pan. Allow them to rest for a few minutes before serving; that's what gives that irresistible crunch!

Serves 4

Ingredients:
1 large brown onion
100g gram flour
1 tsp chaat masala
1 tbsp. dried fenugreek leaf
1 tbsp. coarsely ground coriander seeds
1 tsp salt
1 tsp chilli flakes
2 tsp finely chopped ginger
2 tbsp. fresh coriander and extra to garnish
75ml ice cold soda water/sparkling mineral water

Oil to fry
Karahi to fry in

1. Slice the onion thinly into rings or slice thinly, separate the rings out and set aside. Place the karahi of oil on to heat.

2. Meanwhile, in a separate bowl add the gram flour, chaat masala, dried fenugreek leaves, coarsely ground coriander seeds, salt, chilli flakes, ginger and fresh coriander.

3. Mix well and then slowly add the soda water and whisk to ensure a smooth batter (although it will have plenty of texture with the various spices). You may not need all of the soda water; keep it fairly thick to start with as it will thin rapidly once you mix in the onions and salt.

4. Mix the seasoned batter a spoonful at a time into the sliced onions until the onions are thoroughly coated and can just hold together when you pick them up with a spoon. Don't be tempted to add too much of the flour mixture, otherwise the bhajia will resemble those from a restaurant; use just enough to bind the onions.

5. Test the oil to ensure that the temperature is correct by dropping a small piece of batter into the oil. The batter should sizzle when it hits the oil and then float.

6. Create bhajia the size of a walnut, drop them into the oil and cook them for about 90 seconds and then remove them with a slotted spoon.

7. Garnish with fresh coriander on the serving plate and a squeeze of lemon.

Chef's Tip:

If you have any batter left over, thinly slice some potato (no need to peel), coat the potato slices in the remaining batter and drop into the hot oil for a delicious snack.

Maru Bhajia

Traditional 'naashta' don't get any better than these maru bhajia, simple flavours that provide a very moreish snack to be enjoyed at any time of day. I would recommend my tamarind and date chutney to be served with this dish or perhaps fresh hot salsa chutney would work too! The recipe for the tamarind chutney can be found on page 195.

Serves 4

Ingredients:
400g Maris Piper potatoes
120g gram flour
60g plain flour
1 tsp salt
½ tsp turmeric (optional)
½ tsp red chilli powder
1 tbsp. dried fenugreek leaves
½ green chilli, finely chopped
1 tbsp. finely chopped fresh coriander
Oil to fry in a karahi

A pinch of chaat masala to garnish

1. Wash the potatoes, leave the skin on and slice into thin rounds (the thinner the better). Keep the slices immersed in cold water in a bowl until you're ready to use them.

2. Sieve both the flours into a bowl, add the salt, turmeric, chilli powder, fenugreek leaves, green chilli and coriander and combine the ingredients together.

3. Heat the oil to 'hot' in a karahi or wok. (The trick to get the crispiness of the bhajia is to fry them in hot oil; the potato will cook through, as the slices are quite thin.)

4. Remove two handfuls of potato slices from the water, dry them off in a clean tea towel and put them in a bowl, sprinkle with 4 tablespoons of the flour mixture and mix with your hands to coat the potato slices with the flavoured flour mixture. The moisture from the potatoes should be enough to moisten the flour but if not add a few drops of water from the potatoes.

5. Gently drop the coated potato slices five or six at a time into the heated oil, let them fry for a minute or two, then turn them over and fry for a further minute, until they have a golden hue.

6. Remove onto kitchen towel/absorbent paper using a slotted spoon.

7. To serve, place the bhajia onto individual serving plates, dust with a little chaat masala and serve with a generous helping of a chutney of your choice. Enjoy!

Stuffed Aloo Parathas

Parathas are essentially a type of bread, usually served with a main course dish or as a snack with tea. If you're eating them with a main course, plain parathas will probably suit the dish better, while if you're making them as a flavoursome snack, go for the savoury variety which can be stuffed with different ingredients.

Serves 6-8

To make the paratha dough:
200g chapatti flour
4 tbsp. oil or ghee
½ tsp salt
100ml tepid water – 47°C (this quantity is only a guide; use what you need to bind the flour together)

Equipment:
Whelan (an Indian rolling pin, thin and bevelled and used for rolling breads such as chapatti)
Tawa (a bevelled or flat cast iron cooking griddle) to cook the parathas on

To make the filling:
300g Maris Piper potatoes raw quantity, boiled and mashed very smoothly
Pinch of turmeric
¼ tsp garam masala
1 tsp ginger
¼ tsp green chillies
½ tsp salt
2 tsp fresh coriander
15ml lemon juice

1. Place the flour, oil and salt in a bowl and mix well. Add the water a little at a time as required (as the flour density/grade varies) and knead into a dough. Take a drop of oil and rub it into your hands and knead the dough again to give it a smooth and silken finish. Set aside.

2. For the filling place the mashed potato and all the other filling ingredients into a bowl and mix well. Divide the potato mixture into 10 balls of about 40g each. Set aside.

3. Now come back to the dough and divide into 6-8 balls of about 30g in weight and roll them out evenly to about 4 inches round with the thickness of a £1 coin.

4. Now place the potato ball in the middle of the dough round and lift the edges of the pastry as though it's a dumpling, ensuring that you are cupping the dough round the potato ball, and then bunch the pastry at the top and clip off any excess pastry in the middle.

5. Now gently press down so that the filling spreads through. Be careful it doesn't squelch out though, so don't press too firmly. Gently roll the dough out using very little pressure to about 4 to 5 inches in diameter. Don't place the parathas on top of each other whilst uncooked as they could stick to each other.

6. When you've completed them all, heat the pan and then on a low heat place a paratha on the griddle. Cook for 1 minute before drizzling a little oil around the edges and a little on top. Continue cooking for a further 2 minutes on a low heat before turning over.

7. Cook for another minute before drizzling the oil once again and cook until golden brown.

8. Repeat with the rest of the parathas.

Jhaal Muri

Jhaal muri is a total explosion of flavours and textures which is crunchy, spicy, sweet and sour, thanks to fresh lime juice, cucumber, ginger, onions, tamarind sauce, seve and puffed rice. A special blend of spices is added to season the ingredients which are then finished off with a tamarind sauce and mustard oil.

Serves 4-6

Ingredients:
200g potato boiled, peeled and cut into 1cm cube
150g tomatoes, seeds and centre removed, finely chopped
150g cucumber, seeds removed, cut into ½ cm cubes

Dry ingredients:
280g murmura/muri (puffed rice); buy already puffed
80g fine seve (Bengal gram vermicelli)
80g fried or roasted red skinned peanuts

Wet ingredients & spices:
4 teaspoons mustard oil
2 tsp jhaal muri spice blend (see page 317)
¼ tsp green chilli, finely chopped, adjust to taste
85g cup tamarind paste
½ fresh lime, juiced
2 tbsp. fresh coriander, finely chopped

1. Start by boiling the potatoes and when cooled, peel and cut them into 1cm cubes. Set aside in a large mixing bowl.

2. Finely chop the tomatoes into small pieces – remove the seeds where possible and drain away the juices to avoid making the mixture wet and soggy, and add to the potatoes.

3. Chop the cucumber into ½cm cubes and combine with the tomatoes and potatoes and set aside.

4. Roast the peanuts either in a pan or in the oven until they are golden and toasted. Now combine all the dry ingredients in a separate bowl and set aside.

5. Just as you're ready to serve the dish, mix the dry ingredients with the tomato, potato, cucumber, and the wet ingredients and spices. Toss them together and serve.

6. You may adjust all the ingredients to your taste. Enjoy!

Agni Chilli Chicken Wings

This is a finger licking recipe, and so easy to make it may well become your staple entertaining or BBQ dish. I was reminded of this recipe at a friend's house and wondered how something so pleasing could fall out of my monthly repertoire. The trick is to keep the chicken wings as moist as possible when cooking and if necessary overcook them to ensure that they are easily falling off the bone.

Serves 4

Ingredients:
1 kg chicken wings with some of the skin having been removed

For the marinade:
2 tbsp. oil
1 tbsp. lemon juice
2 tbsp. honey
2 tsp finely chopped garlic
2 tsp finely chopped ginger
1 tsp salt
½ tsp chilli flakes
2 tsp Kashmiri chilli powder
½ tsp hot chilli powder
2 tsp ground cumin

For the garnish:
3 tbsp. sweet chilli sauce
2 tbsp. chopped coriander
2 spring onions – sliced at an angle

1. Start with the marinade for the chicken; make small incisions in the flesh of the wings to enable the marinade to penetrate the surface area. Place all of the ingredients for the marinade in a non-metallic bowl – stir well, taste and season.

2. Add the chicken wings, coat thoroughly and cover with cling film and place in the fridge overnight. Take the chicken wings out of the refrigerator an hour before you are ready to cook them.

3. Place the wings on a tray and put them in the oven at 150°C/gas mark 2 for 50 minutes, cooking slowly to ensure that the wings are soft, succulent and tender. Don't overcrowd the tray – leave 1cm in between each piece of chicken to enable it to crisp up.

4. When the chicken is tender brush the sweet chilli sauce over the pieces and return it to the oven for a further 10 minutes at 220°C/gas mark 7 or place it under the grill.

5. Garnish with chopped coriander and sliced spring onions.

Chef's Tips:

1. Serve with a barbecue or chilli sauce - you will need a finger bowl!

2. If you're not partial to bones, use deboned thigh pieces.

3. Marinate for as long as possible for a deep seated flavour.

Vegetable Pakoras

Crisp, golden and exploding with flavour, these little pakoras are the ultimate party snack. But be warned – your guests will wolf these down as fast as you can fry them! Much like my onion bhajia, these are worlds away from the pakoras that are served in a typical Indian 'curry house' and well worth making as they take very little time to prepare.

Serves 6 as appetizers

Ingredients:
1-2 fresh green or red chillies of medium or mild variety
2 medium red onions
2 medium carrots
1 large potato
1 x 10cm piece of ginger cut into julienne strips
1 large bunch of fresh coriander

1 teaspoon of black mustard seeds
1 heaped teaspoon cumin seeds
1 tsp coarsely ground coriander seeds
½ tsp turmeric
1 ½ tsp salt or 2 tsp sea salt
2 tbsp. lemon or lime juice
100g gram flour (ground chickpea flour) or plain flour if not gram flour

Oil to fry
1 flat-based karahi

1. Finely chop the chillies, slice the red onions, peel and grate the carrots and potato, thinly slice ginger into julienne strips and accumulate everything into a large mixing bowl. Roughly chop the coriander and add it to the mix.

2. Now add the mustard, cumin and coriander seeds, turmeric, salt and lemon juice followed by the gram flour. Mix the ingredients together using your hands and ensure you thoroughly separate all the strands of vegetables to allow the gram flour to coat evenly. The water from the vegetables will begin to release as a result of the salt in the dish. Heat the oil in a karahi.

3. Now create little golf ball size pakoras; don't make them too large otherwise the mixture at the centre won't cook through evenly. Rest them on a large plate or platter until you've finished the mixture by which time the oil may be ready to start frying. Test the oil by adding a small piece of bread to the oil: if it sinks to the bottom and then quickly comes back to the surface the oil is ready. Carefully lift in the pakoras one by one to the oil by hand or using a spoon. Fry the pakoras a few at a time on a medium heat for 2 minutes or until golden brown.

4. Remove the pakoras from the oil, straining them at the side of the vessel to ensure that you have drained as much oil off as possible and set them out onto absorbent paper. Continue until you have used up all the mixture.

5. Serve with some lime wedges, sea salt and beer!

Falafels – Indian Style

Although traditionally associated with Middle Eastern cuisine, falafels are equally delicious when married with Indian spices. The trick to making a great falafel is to use only dried chickpeas (the tinned variety make the mixture too wet) and to include a generous amount of fresh herbs. I also think that what you serve with falafels is important too and these would be great with raitha or my date and tamarind chutney.

Serves 4

Ingredients:
200g dried chickpeas, washed and soaked overnight in boiling water

1 small onion, finely chopped or 4 stalks of spring onions, finely chopped
Handful of chopped fresh coriander
3 garlic cloves, crushed/finely minced
1 tsp ground cumin
1 tsp ground coriander
½ tsp chilli powder
1 tsp salt
2 tsp lemon juice
1 tsp bicarbonate of soda

Oil to fry in a karahi

1. Soak the chickpeas in boiling water overnight.

2. Rinse the chickpeas in fresh cold water and set aside to drain for at least 10 minutes.

3. Now place the chickpeas, finely chopped onion, fresh coriander, garlic, ground cumin, ground coriander, chilli powder, salt, lemon juice and bicarbonate of soda into a food processor. Blitz until broken down into a smooth filling.

4. Mould the mixture into pieces the size and shape of a golf ball and then flatten it into oval patties.

5. Heat the oil in a karahi and when the oil is up to temperature fry the falafels on a medium heat for 2-3 minutes on each side, until golden brown and firm. Serve hot or cold with a tamarind or mint chutney. You could also serve with a couscous salad or load into a pitta bread/wrap with a salad of choice.

Serving Tip:
This dish is a great accompaniment to barbecues – serve with a yoghurt dip.

Savoury Potato Truffles

'Great balls of deliciousness': this is the only way to describe this classic street food dish. They might also be otherwise known as 'batata vada', but in my usual way I've sassed up the recipe a bit with a lighter, fluffy potato mixture to make them truffle-like, and made the batter mixture much thinner than you might ordinarily find.

Serves 4 as canapés/starter

Ingredients:
500g mashed potato made from a firm potato (King Edwards)
1 tbsp. broken cashew nut pieces
1 tbsp. yellow raisins
2 tbsp. lemon juice
1 tsp salt
1 tsp sesame seeds
1 tsp freshly chopped ginger
¼ tsp garam masala
¼ tsp finely chopped green chillies
½ tsp ground cumin
Pinch turmeric
1 large handful chopped fresh coriander

For the batter:
100g gram flour
⅛ tsp chilli powder
½ tsp roughly crushed coriander seeds
⅛ tsp salt
⅛ tsp turmeric
1 tbsp. probiotic yoghurt
Warm water to loosen batter
½ tsp bicarbonate of soda

1 litre oil to fry

1. Start by scrubbing the potatoes with a vegetable brush, then halve or quarter the potatoes depending on their size. Boil the potatoes in salted water until they are cooked and suitable for mashing. Drain the potatoes and allow them to cool before peeling off the skin and mashing into a smooth consistency (do not add any butter or milk). Boiling the potatoes with the skin on will prevent the potatoes from becoming too waterlogged which is important for the consistency of the mash.

2. Meanwhile break up the cashew nuts into small pieces about ¼cm in size and set aside. Soak the yellow raisins in boiling water for about 5 minutes to rehydrate, then drain and set aside.

3. Whilst the potatoes are still warm add the lemon juice, salt, cashew nuts, sesame seeds, raisins, ginger, garam masala, fresh green chilli, cumin, turmeric and fresh coriander. Mix well until all of the spices are combined, but mix gently to avoid softening the potato too much. Set aside in the fridge, time permitting (this mix can be made the day before to allow the spices to soak into the potato).

4. Whilst the potatoes are cooling make the batter by sieving the gram flour into a large mixing bowl, and adding the chilli powder, roughly crushed coriander seeds, salt, turmeric and yoghurt. Mix well and add 1 tablespoon of water at a time to loosen the consistency into a thick but pourable batter. Heat the oil in a karahi or wok and in the meantime roll the mixture into walnut sized balls and lay out on a plate ready to coat in batter before frying.

5. Just before frying add ½ teaspoon of bicarbonate of soda to the batter, mix well and dip the potato balls into the batter and place into the hot oil. Fry for about 2 minutes until lightly golden brown and the batter is completely crispy. Remove from the karahi with a slotted spoon and rest on the spoon to allow them to air dry before placing onto absorbent paper to take up any excess oil.

6. Serve with tamarind sauce and enjoy!

Main Course Meat

When you think of Indian food, what is the first dish that springs to mind? For most people it is a curry, a dish so ubiquitous in this country, it almost feels as British as bangers and mash. The funny thing is, 'curry' as we have come to know it doesn't actually exist in India! It's very much an English thing.

In my classes we talk about curries as our customers would know them and I find the best way to describe a curry is either a sauce-based dish or an Indian casserole. I realise I've suddenly made the dish seem somewhat less appealing but suddenly the idea of cooking a curry seems remarkably less daunting.

The local Indian restaurants haven't helped matters over the years as they've tried to produce what they think the average English consumers want, and have continued along a theme for such a long time that it's been difficult to break through the mould so as not to confuse their customers. For example a chicken jalfrezi is essentially labelled as a curry, as one might an aloo gobi. Yet neither can be called a curry: one is essentially a chicken stir-fry and the other a dry vegetable dish – usually referred to as a *subzi* the Hindi word to describe cooked vegetable dishes.

The art of a good curry is the holy grail of Indian cooking: when you master this technique, you'll have the confidence to venture into more complicated dishes.

So what it is that defines a curry? Well, a sauce-based dish relies upon a thickening agent of some kind, often caramelized onions, combined with tomatoes, perhaps. Yoghurt or gram flour is also commonly used to create sauces, as are ground cashew nuts or peanuts depending on regional differences.

The most important thing to remember when creating a curry is to allow the base ingredients, i.e. the onions or tomatoes, to cook down slowly to lose the acidity and moisture and bind together, creating a truly integrated sauce. This becomes the base

for a sauce even without the spices. As the onions begin to sweat in the pan it is essential that you do this on a low heat to avoid colouring the onions before releasing the moisture.

This is where many people are inclined to take a short cut and crank the heat up, assuming that the object of the exercise is simply to brown the onions. However in doing so the onions will not soften as they should and you are likely to retain too much of the bitter acidic flavour within the onion, ending up with crunchy onions that won't bind together to create a cohesive sauce.

So in other words time is the key ingredient – you can't rush a good sauce; whether it's a curry, or a good Italian ragu, the best flavours come from being patient and allowing the ingredients to cook out properly. That's not to say that curries are a long time in the making; it's perfectly possible to make a quick curry, but you need to take your time over the most essential steps. Even as you add the spices, allow a few minutes of cooking in between each step to give the ingredients time to acquaint 'themselves' with one another in the pan.

Through the recipes in these chapters, I hope you will discover how much variety there is when it comes to Indian main courses. There is so much more than what we think of as curry or 'going for an Indian'. From beautifully cooked seafood to gorgeous spring lamb, there are dishes here to enjoy all year round.

Masala Chicken

This simple, flavoursome chicken recipe is a mid-week winner in many Indian homes. A popular and reliable dish, keep it in your repertoire in the same way you do a hearty spag bol. There are a few tricks of the trade to bear in mind too. If you add some cubed potatoes to the recipe, it will make the dish go much further and the flavours from the chicken and spices make the potatoes quite delicious. For a vegetarian alternative, you can simply swap in some Quorn, tofu, paneer or whatever vegetables take your fancy in place of the chicken. If you want to boost the mineral content, try adding finely chopped spinach at the end of the cooking process.

Serves 4

Ingredients:
600g chicken thighs, deboned and de-skinned, cut into 1 inch chunks
3 tbsp. oil
2 cloves
2 cardamom pods
2 cinnamon sticks
2 bay leaves
2 medium onions, finely chopped (200g)
3 tsp finely chopped garlic
3 tsp finely chopped ginger
½ tsp hot chilli powder
¾ tsp turmeric
1½ tsp ground cumin
1½ tsp ground coriander
¼ tsp garam masala
1 tsp salt, or to taste
2 x 3-finger pinches of fresh coriander for cooking and garnish
150g tinned chopped tomatoes
75ml hot water or to desired consistency

Pinch of garam masala to garnish

1. Heat the oil in a deep pan, then lower the heat before adding the whole spices to avoid browning them too much. Fry the whole spices – cloves, cardamoms and cinnamon sticks – for 5 seconds. Then add the bay leaves together with the onions and fry until soft and light brown in colour on a low heat to ensure the onions soften before they colour and caramelize. This should take up to 10-12 minutes on a low temperature. When the onions have lost their texture and are translucent, add the garlic and ginger and cook for a further 2 minutes continuing with a low temperature to avoid overcooking the hot herbs (garlic and ginger).

2. Now add the chilli powder, turmeric, ground cumin, ground coriander, salt, garam masala, and a 3-finger pinch of the fresh coriander to the onions, and stir well to ensure that they are thoroughly integrated. Cook on a low heat for 5 minutes to allow the essential oils to release from the spices.

3. Add the chicken, turn up the heat to medium and mix well to ensure that all the spices have coated the chicken and it is beginning to seal. Lower the heat once the chicken is sizzling, then cook for 3-4 minutes with the lid on.

4. Add the tomatoes, turn the heat up to medium and stir in. Once the temperature is back to a simmer, turn the heat to low once again and cook for a further 7-8 minutes with the lid on.

5. Now add the hot water. You may not need all of it, so add the water based on the sauce consistency you would like. Bring to the boil and then reduce the temperature, replace the lid and cook for 5-10 minutes or until the chicken is cooked.

6. Garnish with the remaining fresh coriander and a pinch of garam masala. Serve immediately with hot chapattis or rotis and rice.

Chicken Tikka Masala

Don't be put off by the rather long ingredients list in this recipe; it is a step-by-step process that will pay handsome dividends in its flavour, intensity and compliments. The marinade in this recipe is equally transferable for use with prawns, lamb or beef to great effect.

Serves 4

Ingredients:
750g chicken thigh fillets – cut into bite sized pieces

For the chicken marinade:
50g natural yoghurt
1 tbsp. oil
1 tsp salt
2 tsp garlic + 2 tsp ginger
1 tbsp. lemon juice
2 tsp paprika
¼ tsp turmeric
½ tsp red chilli powder
2 tsp ground cumin + 1 tsp ground coriander
1 tbsp. fresh coriander

For the sauce:
4 tbsp. oil
3 cinnamon sticks + 4 bay leaves
4 green cardamoms
2 medium onions finely chopped
2 tsp garlic + 2 tsp ginger
400g tin of chopped tomatoes
½ tsp chopped green chillies
1 tsp dried mango powder (amchoor)
½ tsp salt
2 tsp ground cumin + 2 tsp ground coriander
1 tbsp. fresh coriander – for the spice mix
100ml of fresh cream or crème fraîche
1 tbsp. jaggery + 1 tbsp. tomato puree
1 tbsp. lemon juice
100ml water as required – you may prefer the sauce to be less viscous
1 tbsp. fresh coriander to garnish and to serve
¼ tsp garam masala to garnish

1. Firstly make the marinade. Place all the ingredients for the marinade in a large bowl and mix well. Add the chicken and rub the marinade into the chicken thoroughly. Leave to marinate for 24 hours preferably, or at least for a few hours. Then place the contents on a baking tray and cook in the oven for 25 minutes at 180°C/gas mark 4. Spread the chicken out across the tray and avoid the pieces touching each other to avoid them boiling on the tray.

2. To create the sauce, heat the oil in a in large-based pan and add the cinnamon, cardamom and bay leaves before adding the onions, and sauté for 20 minutes over a low heat to cook out the water from the onions until they are lightly golden brown.

3. Add the garlic and ginger and infuse for a few minutes before adding the tomatoes. Increase the temperature, bringing up to a simmer, then lower the heat and cook with the lid on for a further 10 minutes or until all the water has evaporated and the acidity of the tomatoes has cooked out. Ensure you do not let the water from the lid fall into the pan at any time.

4. Now for the spices: add the green chillies, dried mango powder, salt, ground cumin and ground coriander to the sauce. Add the fresh coriander and mix well, then cook for 10 minutes on a low heat with the lid on before adding the cream or crème fraîche and stir once again. Now add the jaggery, tomato puree and lemon juice and stir once again.

5. When the chicken is cooked add it to the pan; scrape the baking tray well and add to the sauce. Stir through and add as much of the water as necessary to achieve the desired consistency. Cook for 5 minutes until the chicken and sauce are well integrated.

6. Garnish with fresh coriander and garam masala to taste and serve at once.

Chicken Ghee Roast

This is a south Indian recipe introduced to me by Pooja, a very talented chef here at the Academy, and originates from Mangalore on the western coast of south India between Goa and Kerala. It is usually eaten with crispy rotis made from rice flour, which is a traditional south Indian bread.

Serves 4

Ingredients:
600g boneless chicken thighs, cut into bite sized pieces

4 tbsp. yoghurt
1 tsp turmeric powder
2 tbsp. lemon juice
1 tsp salt
2 hot dry red chillies
3 Kashmiri dry red chillies
3 tbsp. ghee
½ tsp cumin seeds
½ tbsp. coriander seeds
¼ tsp fenugreek seeds
2 cloves
2 black peppercorns
5 garlic cloves
1 inch finely grated ginger
2 tbsp. desiccated coconut
1 tbsp. tamarind paste
1 tsp mustard seeds
A handful of curry leaves
1 tsp jaggery

1. Mix the yoghurt, turmeric, lemon juice and salt in a bowl. Add the chicken and marinate for at least 30 minutes or more, time permitting.

2. Meanwhile to make the spice paste, dry roast the hot dry red chillies and the Kashmiri chillies in a pan on a low heat for 1-2 minutes until they are aromatic. Remove from the pan and set aside. In the same pan add a teaspoon of ghee and then add the cumin, coriander and fenugreek seeds, cloves and peppercorns. Gently infuse in the warm ghee until they are aromatic. Remove from the heat and set aside to cool.

3. Transfer the chillies and the cooled spices along with the garlic, ginger, coconut and tamarind paste to a mortar and pestle or a mini food processor if you prefer. Add a teaspoon of water if needed to make it into a smooth paste.

4. Now add 2 tablespoons of ghee into a heavy-based pan, add the marinated chicken and cook on a gentle heat until golden brown. Set it aside.

5. Add remaining 2 teaspoons of ghee into a heavy-based pan, add the mustard seeds, and wait until they have finished popping before adding the curry leaves followed by the spice paste and bring to a gentle simmer. Cook for 5-6 minutes on a low heat to cook out the tamarind and coconut.

6. Add the cooked chicken along with any juices into the pan and the jaggery, and mix well to coat the chicken with the spices. Place the lid on and continue to cook for 5 minutes on a low heat.

7. Garnish with more curry leaves on top and serve hot with rice or chapattis.

Chef's Tip:

The dish is meant to be dry and not saucy so refrain from adding water once it is cooking.

Lamb Biriyani

Biriyani originates from Persia, more specifically Iran, and relates to rice that has been fried first. It was brought to India by the Moghuls and was cooked over charcoal in an earthen pot or even buried in the hot midday sun to cook underground. Biriyani has always been a bit of a luxury in the food sense, reserved for special occasions or a family celebration. Whilst the ingredients themselves are really no different to any other meat and rice dish, bringing the two elements together and cooking over a longer period of time develops a very different flavour that is altogether special.

Serves 4

Ingredients:
1kg lamb shoulder, chopped into bite sized pieces

2 small fresh red chillies, finely chopped
2 tsp ground coriander
2 tsp ground cumin
1 tsp salt
½ tsp garam masala
1 tsp ground turmeric
2 tbsp. white vinegar
Handful of finely chopped coriander
100g natural yoghurt

400g basmati rice
2 tbsp. ghee
2 cinnamon sticks
4 cardamom pods, bruised
6 cloves
3 bay leaves
2 large onions, thinly sliced
500ml lamb stock
200g frozen peas
50g currants

For the garnish:
50g sliced almonds – toasted
2-3 tbsp. fresh coriander leaves – finely chopped
2 medium tomatoes, quartered, deseeded and cut into cubes
Seeds from ½ a pomegranate
Pinch of garam masala

1. Start by trimming the lamb of any excess fat or sinew and then cut it into bite sized pieces. Set aside. Combine the chillies, ground coriander, cumin, salt, garam masala, turmeric, vinegar, fresh coriander and yoghurt in a medium bowl and mix well. Add the lamb and ensure that all of the pieces are well coated. Cover and refrigerate for an hour.

2. Meanwhile, place the rice in a large bowl and wash in warm water several times until the water runs clear. Cover with warm water and stand for 30 minutes. Drain well when ready to use.

3. Heat the ghee in a large pan then add the cinnamon sticks, cardamom pods, cloves and bay leaves followed by the onions and cook on a low heat until they are golden brown.

4. Add the seasoned lamb; stir well, increase the temperature and bring to a simmer. Reduce the temperature, cover with a tight lid and cook on a low heat for about 1-1½ hours or until the lamb is tender, stirring occasionally. Although you may be tempted to add a little water, the lamb and yoghurt should release sufficient moisture to cook the meat tenderly – do ensure that the temperature is very low. However if the meat is becoming dry add 75ml of water halfway through cooking the lamb.

5. Alternatively the lamb can be cooked in the oven on gas mark 2/150°C in a covered casserole dish for 2 hours or until the meat is tender. Next stir the rice into the lamb and cook on the hob for 5-8 minutes until the rice is dry frying with the lamb.

6. Now add the hot stock into the rice and lamb mixture and bring to the boil. Lower the temperature and cook for 10 minutes on a very low heat until all of the moisture has evaporated.

7. Stir in the peas and currants; stand, covered, for 10 minutes. To serve, garnish with the toasted almonds, fresh coriander, tomatoes, pomegranate seeds and a final pinch of garam masala. Remove the cinnamon sticks, bay leaves and cardamoms if visible. Serve with some seasoned natural yoghurt.

A Good Ole Jalfrezi

Jalfrezi simply means 'to stir-fry' so to make this dish you want to cook with a heavy-based wok or stir-fry pan. The flavours in this recipe are rich and strong; it is a hearty dish and will clear the cobwebs with great use of all the hot herbs and vegetables. It's always worth making a little extra; the leftovers, should there be any, will be well received the next day. The recipe works just as well with red meat, though the cooking times will need to be adjusted.

Serves 4

Ingredients:
3 tbsp. oil
5 cardamom pods
8 whole cloves
3 bay leaves
2 medium onions, finely chopped
700g skinless chicken pieces, approx 1 inch square
5 tsp garlic, finely chopped
4 tsp finely chopped ginger
1 tsp turmeric
1 tsp ground cumin
2 tsp ground coriander
2 green finger chillies finely chopped or 1 tsp hot chilli powder, or to taste
1 tsp salt or to taste
½ tsp ground black pepper
6 medium tomatoes, chopped or 1 x 400g can of chopped tomatoes
Chopped fresh coriander, to garnish and to spice

½ tbsp. oil
1 green and 1 red pepper cut into strips
½ tsp finely chopped garlic
½ tsp garam masala

1. Heat the 3 tablespoons of oil in a large pan over a low to medium heat. Add the cardamom pods and whole cloves and sauté for a few seconds before adding the bay leaves. Now add the chopped onions immediately on top of the bay as they will brown very quickly. Cook until the onions are soft and have lost their texture.

2. Add the chicken pieces to the pan, increase the temperature and cook to seal and colour the chicken on all sides. When the chicken has almost completely browned, add the garlic, ginger, turmeric, ground cumin and coriander, chilli powder (or fresh chilli), salt and pepper. Cook for 5 minutes on a low temperature to allow the spices to yield their flavours.

3. Now add the chopped tomatoes and 1 tablespoon of fresh coriander and once it reaches simmering point reduce the temperature to maintain a gentle simmer. Cover the pan and simmer for 30 minutes.

4. In a separate shallow frying pan heat ½ a tablespoon of oil and add the red and green peppers as well as ½ teaspoon finely chopped garlic. Stir-fry together to give a little colour to the peppers and slightly soften. Remove from the heat and add to the chicken dish along with the garam masala. Stir well and continue to simmer for another 5 minutes with the lid on. Once the chicken is tender and juicy switch off the heat.

5. Garnish with coriander and garam masala.

Chef's Tip:

The flavours will intensify beautifully if the dish is made 24 hours ahead. However I would recommend you stop at the point where you've cooked the chicken. Prepare the pan-fried peppers just before you're about to serve the dish.

Lamb Raan – Spice-Braised Shoulder of Lamb

Although the recipe calls for lamb, feel free to use mutton, or even goat; both are hugely underused yet have such great qualities as meat, providing depth of flavour. The shoulder joint is much preferred from a taste and texture viewpoint and the slow cooking process will render the fat away from the shoulder joint if you feel that shoulder is fattier than leg. However, the leg does look more attractive from a presentation point of view, especially if the dish is going to be a centrepiece, and by the time you've finished all the garnishing it really is designed to be a dish to impress.

Serves 4

Ingredients:

To make the marinade:
2 tbsp. oil
25ml malt vinegar
4 tbsp. plain yoghurt
1 tbsp. rose water
1½ tsp finely chopped ginger
1½ tsp finely chopped garlic
1 tsp salt
½ tsp hot chilli powder
50g pre-fried onions
1 tsp cumin seeds
2 tsp ground cumin
2 tsp ground coriander
1 tbsp. fresh coriander, stalks and leaves

For the lamb:
1 shoulder or leg of lamb, weighing about 1.5kg, trimmed of any surface fat
Extra oil to grease the roasting tray
4 large potatoes, peeled and sliced 2cm thick
3 bay leaves
2 cinnamon sticks, each about 5cm long
3 green cardamom pods
200ml chicken or lamb stock
2 tbsp. melted butter
2 tsp lemon juice
A pinch of chaat masala
1 tbsp. chopped fresh coriander leaves and stalks
200ml double cream for the gravy
¼ tsp garam masala

For the roux:
25g plain flour and 25g butter – mixed together to a smooth paste

1. With the tip of a sharp knife, cut small incisions in the lamb shoulder at approximately 5cm intervals. In a separate bowl mix together the oil, vinegar, yoghurt, rose water, ginger, garlic, salt, hot chilli powder, fried onions, cumin seeds, ground cumin and coriander and fresh coriander. Create a thick paste and using your hands, massage the spice mixture over the shoulder, rubbing and pressing the spices into the gashes created by the knife.

2. Set aside for a few hours or preferably overnight. Arrange the sliced potato on a deep, well-oiled baking tray. Place the shoulder on top (create a stack) and the bay leaves, cinnamon and cardamom, then pour 200ml chicken or lamb stock around the shoulder.

3. Cover the tray with foil very tightly. Place in oven preheated to 160°C/gas mark 3 and braise for 4 hours until the meat is very tender and ready to fall off the bone. Drain off any liquids as you would with a roasting tray. Pass these liquids through a sieve and reserve to make a jus.

4. Now roast the shoulder on a barbecue or under a very hot grill, basting with the melted butter, until crisp. Finish with a drizzle of lemon juice, any left-over melted butter, a pinch of chaat masala, more pre-fried onions and freshly chopped coriander.

5. Optional – For the sauce, bring the cooking juices to the boil in a small pan and simmer until reduced to a coating consistency. If the sauce is too runny add a small piece of the roux at a time, whisking vigorously until it is incorporated and the sauce has thickened sufficiently. Correct the seasoning and gradually stir in the cream, garam masala and more fresh coriander.

6. Pour the sauce over the meat and serve with cumin-fragrant basmati rice or flatbreads. For a delicious accompaniment serve with seasoned yoghurt or raita. The potatoes should be served with the lamb – they will be very tender but taste delicious.

Chicken Pathia

This recipe comes from my family hometown in Gujarat, influenced largely by our Parsi friends and neighbours that served this dish on big celebratory occasions. Pathia recipes are distinguished by their sweet and sour flavours which I have achieved in this recipe with the liberal use of lime juice and tamarind and then balanced with the delightful jaggery and a dollop of mango chutney.

Serves 4

Ingredients:
600g chicken thigh fillets diced into 1 inch chunks
¼ tsp ground turmeric
1 pinch of salt for marinade + 1 tsp salt
1 tsp cumin seeds
1 tsp black mustard seeds
½ tsp black peppercorns
5 tsp finely grated garlic
2 tbsp. lime juice
3 tbsp. oil
4 cardamom pods
1 bay leaf
1 onion (about 220g), very finely diced
200g tinned tomatoes
1 heaped tbsp. tomato puree
½ tsp Kashmiri chilli powder
1 tsp paprika
1 tsp dried fenugreek leaves
1 tsp ground coriander
8-10 curry leaves (fresh if possible, if not use dried)
50-200ml water to required consistency
2 tsp jaggery
½ tsp tamarind paste
1 tbsp. smooth mango chutney

For the garnish:
¼ tsp garam masala
2 tbsp. fresh coriander
A squeeze of lemon juice

1. Marinate the chicken in a bowl with the turmeric and a pinch of salt.

2. Grind the cumin, mustard seeds and black peppercorns coarsely then add the garlic and lime juice and blitz to a thick paste in a food processor (add a little water if needed).

3. Heat the oil in a saucepan over a medium heat. Add the cardamom pods and bay leaf and sizzle for a few seconds. Then add the onion and sauté on a low heat until it is very soft and translucent (this can take up to 20 minutes). Now add the paste and cook for 2 minutes, stirring well to make sure that it doesn't stick to the pan.

4. Add the tomatoes and tomato puree and cook for a further 5 minutes until the tomatoes begin to soften and the oil starts to separate from the tomatoes.

5. Now add the chilli powder, paprika, fenugreek leaves, 1 teaspoon of salt and ground coriander and stir for a further 2 minutes. Stir in the curry leaves then add the chicken, and cook, stirring occasionally for 20 minutes or until the chicken is cooked through. Then add as much water as required to achieve your desired consistency, the jaggery, tamarind paste and mango chutney. Mix well and simmer over a low heat for a further 10 minutes.

6. Turn off the heat, stir in the garam masala and finish with the chopped coriander and the lemon juice. Enjoy with hot naan bread or fresh chapattis.

Keema

This is another classic weekday recipe, best served with hot chapatti or naan bread. It is as common in Indian meat-eating households as shepherd's pie is in British homes. This dish will make you see potatoes in a new light. Far from being used to simply 'bulk out' a meal, they are irresistible when cooked in the sauce with the minced lamb. A quick tip: if you want a thicker sauce, don't add the water until almost at the end. Wait to see how much water is released from the meat and the potatoes and then add a little at a time until you reach the desired consistency.

Serves 4

Ingredients:
2 tbsp. oil
4 green cardamom pods
4 cloves
2 cinnamon sticks
1 giant black cardamom
1 medium onion, finely chopped
200g chopped tinned tomatoes
500g very lean minced lamb
2 tsp finely chopped garlic
2 tsp finely chopped ginger
1 tsp hot chilli powder
1 tsp turmeric
2 tsp roasted ground cumin
½ tsp garam masala
2 tsp salt
2 medium sized potatoes cut into chunks
200ml hot water
8 strands of fresh coriander, chopped
1 tsp lemon juice

1. Heat the oil in a non-stick pan and when hot add the whole dry spices: green cardamom pods, cloves, cinnamon and giant cardamom. Sizzle for a few seconds, then add the onion and fry, stirring for a few minutes until it is just beginning to turn brown.

2. Add the tomatoes and cook on a medium heat until the water has evaporated and the oil is separating.

3. Now add the lamb. Use the back of the wooden spoon to break down the morsels of meat to prevent it from being lumpy.

4. Add the garlic, ginger, chilli powder, turmeric, cumin, garam masala and salt. Stir well to ensure that the spices blend into the lamb and cook for 10 minutes.

5. Add the potatoes and the water to the pan and stir well. Cover with the lid and simmer gently for 10 minutes or until the potatoes are cooked.

6. Remove from the heat, garnish with the freshly chopped coriander and lemon juice and serve with chapattis or naan bread.

Methi Chicken

Methi is one of my favourite ingredients! It think it can embellish the flavour of almost anything and that's certainly what I think it achieves in this dish, taking a simple spicing process and creating a completely different flavour profile. Methi is bitter in taste and considered to be a powerful herb so nutritionally speaking it competes with spinach for its rich source of iron, vitamin K and fibre. Methi is one of the oldest herbs, and is said to have been around for over 6,000 years. Its Latin name, fenugreek, means Greek hay.

Serves 4

Ingredients:
4 tbsp. oil
1 cinnamon stick
3 cloves
3 green cardamoms
1 tsp cumin seeds
1 medium onion – very finely diced
3 tsp garlic – finely minced
3 tsp ginger – finely chopped
1 bunch of fresh methi (fenugreek) – leaves only, washed and finely chopped
600g chicken thigh cut into 1 inch chunks
1 tsp salt
1 tsp turmeric
½ tsp chilli powder
2 tsp ground roasted cumin
2 tsp ground coriander
¼ tsp garam masala
50ml hot water
2 tbsp. chopped coriander
Lemon juice for drizzling

1. In a deep saucepan heat the oil, then add the cinnamon stick, cloves and green cardamoms and sizzle for a few seconds before adding the cumin seeds followed by the onion. Cook for 2-3 minutes on a gentle heat.

2. Now add the garlic, ginger and fresh methi leaves. Stir well and cook for 2 minutes to allow the flavours to infuse.

3. Add the chicken, increasing the temperature a little temporarily until the heat is soaked up by the chicken and it is beginning to seal; this should only take 3 to 4 minutes.

4. Reduce the temperature back to low to maintain a gentle sizzle whilst adding all the dry spices: salt, turmeric, chilli powder, cumin, coriander and garam masala. Stir well to ensure that all the spices are thoroughly mixed into the chicken. Once the chicken is gently simmering, cook on a low temperature with the lid on for about 10 minutes to allow the infusion of flavours. After 10 minutes a sauce should be developing as water is releasing from the chicken and methi leaves.

5. Add 50ml of hot water or as much water as you would like to take the consistency to your preference. Taste to check the seasoning to your taste. Continue to cook until the chicken is tender and cooked through.

6. Garnish with 2 tablespoons of chopped coriander and drizzle a little lemon juice over the chicken.

7. Serve with a bread of your choice or some pilaf rice.

Lamb Chops

There is no doubt in my mind that lamb tastes best when it has been marinated. Any type of marinade can transform an inexpensive cut of lamb into a tender and juicy treat. The recipe for marinated and grilled lamb chops is one of my favourites when entertaining and for BBQs. You can make it on the grill, hob or even in a crockpot or slow cooker. Serve it with Middle Eastern pilaf rice, homemade spicy potato wedges or with a salad for a low carb meal.

As an aside, you can also make them in a slow cooker if you have one, cooking on a low temperature for 8 hours. The slow cooker really makes the meat tender and gives the spices time to soak into the lamb fully.

Serves 4

Ingredients:
1kg lamb chops

For the marinade
3 tbsp. oil
½ tsp black pepper
½ tsp salt or to taste
1 tsp ground coriander
1 tsp ground cumin
3 cloves garlic, finely chopped
1 cardamom pod, seeds removed and ground in a mortar and pestle
1 tbsp. natural yoghurt
2 tablespoons lemon juice

For the garnish
Fresh coriander, chopped
Lemon wedge for squeezing

1. Combine the ingredients for the marinade in a medium bowl. Add the lamb chops, rub the marinade into the chops and set aside for at least an hour at room temperature or preferably for up to 24 hours in the fridge, tightly cling-filmed to keep the flavours within the bowl.

2. When ready to use, preheat the grill and cook on a tray for 5-7 minutes on each side.

3. Garnish with coriander and a squeeze of lemon juice. Enjoy!

Lamb Rogan Josh

One of the Mughals' favourite destinations during the hot summers was the mountainous regions of Kashmir. There, they escaped from the unrelenting heat of the plains. The presence of the Mughals encouraged a blossoming of Kashmiri cuisine and it was here that this all too familiar dish was perfected.

Dishes such as rogan josh are strictly regional and therefore would not be a staple dish throughout the Indian subcontinent. The British restaurant proprietors hailed originally from Kashmir and the Bengal regions of India and thus such dishes have become woven into the fabric of Indian restaurant menus.

Serves 4

Ingredients:
4 tbsp. oil (2 tbsp. + 2 tbsp.)
500g lamb shoulder diced into 2cm cubes
2 cinnamon sticks
3 whole cardamom pods – popped
4 cloves
4 black peppercorns
4 bay leaves
1 large onion finely diced
3 tsp garlic – finely chopped/ minced
3 tsp ginger finely chopped
3 tsp ground coriander
3 tsp ground cumin
1 tsp hot chilli powder
1 tsp turmeric
1 tsp salt
5 tbsp. plain yoghurt
300ml hot water or as much as you prefer
½ tsp garam masala
2 tbsp. fresh coriander – finely chopped

Optional:
2 whole red chillies to garnish
10 fried curry leaves to garnish

1. In a large deep sauté pan or skillet, heat half of the oil and brown the meat on all sides. Don't be tempted to rush this stage! If the pan does not have a large surface area, do this in small batches so that the meat sears evenly. If you try to brown too much at one time, the juices will leach out of the meat and boil rather than brown and seal. As the meat browns, remove it to a separate bowl and continue until all of the meat is browned.

2. Add the remaining 2 tablespoons of oil to the pan used to brown the meat. Heat the oil and add the cinnamon sticks, cardamom pods, cloves, peppercorns, and bay leaves.

3. Add the onion, stir well and cook on a low heat for about 15 minutes or until it has softened, and turned lightly golden in colour.

4. Add the garlic and ginger, stir and cook for 2-3 minutes, before adding the dry spices: coriander, cumin, chilli powder, turmeric and salt and mix together.

5. Now add the meat back to the pan as well as the juices, stir and then begin to add the yoghurt 1 tablespoon at a time, blending well before you add the next spoonful. If you rush this process the yoghurt could split. Bring up to a simmer and cook for about 10 minutes.

6. Add the water and mix well. Bring to a boil, scraping all the browned spices off the bottom of the pan. Lower the heat, cover with a tight fitting lid and simmer for at least 2-3 hours or until the meat is tender. Stir every 15 minutes or so during the process. Alternatively transfer to a casserole dish and cook at 160°C for 3 hours. I prefer this method as it tends to keep all the flavours in the pan and I can get on with other dishes. Stir in the garam masala and finish with the fresh coriander, fresh chillies and curry leaves.

Spicy Ceylonese Coconut Chicken

The generous use of hot herbs in this dish cuts through the richness of the coconut, without undermining it, which is key since it is the coconut milk that differentiates the dish from so many others, providing a new range of flavours from old Ceylonese India.

Serves 4

Ingredients:
600g boneless chicken thigh meat, cut into bite sized pieces

Marinade for chicken:
1½ tbsp. oil
3 tbsp. lemon juice
2 heaped tsp garlic
4 tbsp. creamed coconut
¾ tsp salt
¾ tsp of red chilli powder
2 tsp ground cumin
2 tbsp. fresh coriander

Sauce:
2½ tbsp. oil
2 medium onions (300g raw), finely chopped
3 tsp garlic
2 tsp ginger
¾ tsp turmeric
2 tsp ground coriander
1½ tsp ground cumin
¾ tsp red chilli powder
1 tsp jaggery
1 chicken stock cube
3 tbsp. of fresh coriander – 2 at the time of spices/1 at garnishing
300ml coconut milk

1. Place all the marinade ingredients starting with the wet ingredients in a bowl and mix well.

2. Add chicken and mix thoroughly so the chicken is evenly coated with the marinade. Set aside at room temperature for an hour or in the fridge overnight. Place the chicken on an oven tray and cook for 20-25 minutes at 180°C/gas mark 4.

3. While the chicken is in the oven, heat the oil in a pan, add the finely chopped onions and caramelize very slowly into a golden brown colour. This should take about 15 minutes.

4. Add the garlic and ginger and mix through; cook for 2 minutes on a low heat to allow the flavours and aromas to infuse the onions.

5. Add the turmeric, ground coriander, ground cumin, red chilli powder, jaggery, the stock cube and 1 tablespoon of the fresh coriander and stir into the onions. Allow the flavours to develop for a few minutes.

6. Turn up the heat, add the coconut milk and stir through using the back of the wooden spoon to integrate the spices into the coconut milk, then reduce the heat back to very low and cook for approx 3-5 minutes.

7. Add the cooked chicken and any water or sauces from the chicken tray to the sauce base, mix well and simmer gently for a few minutes. Add further water to loosen the sauce to the desired thickness when you are ready to reheat.

Cinnamon Spring Lamb

No! Stop! Don't look at the ingredients list for this dish and faint! It actually reads like a list of the super-rich of the spice world, all working to empower the lamb with ever more goodness. The early spicing process with the whole spices infuses the oil with the essential oils that then go on to transfer the flavours into the onions and then the lamb.

Serves 4

Ingredients:
400g lean spring lamb cubed into 1 inch cubes
4 tbsp. oil (2 tbsp. + 2 tbsp.)
1 black cardamom
2 green cardamoms
1 x 4 inch piece of cinnamon bark
3 cloves
2 bay leaves
200g finely chopped onions
2 tsp chopped garlic
2 tsp ginger
2 tsp ground coriander
2½ tsp ground cumin
½ tsp ground cinnamon powder
½ tsp turmeric
1 tsp salt
½ tsp red chilli powder
2 x 3-finger pinch of coriander
200g chopped tinned tomatoes
300-400ml water
Heaped tsp tomato puree (optional)

For the garnish:
1 piece of ginger shredded into julienne
Fresh coriander- chopped
¼ tsp garam masala
Lemon juice to garnish

Chef's Tip:

The sauce created by the meat juices and slowly caramelized onions lends itself to vegetables so you could add potatoes, swede or even lentils for the last 20 minutes' cooking time to get a wonderful one pot Indian casserole.

1. Heat the oil in a deep pan and then add cardamoms, cinnamon bark, cloves and bay leaves for 5 seconds, before adding the onions and sauté until a golden brown caramelized colour and the water has evaporated. This is a slow process (20-25 minutes) and it should be cooked on a low heat. You will need to stir now and then, but if you're using a lid then ensure you don't allow the water to fall into the pan. Add garlic and ginger and cook for a further 5 minutes on a low heat. Add the dry spices of ground coriander, ground cumin, cinnamon powder, turmeric, salt, red chilli powder and the fresh coriander. Stir in the spices and once again cook for 5 minutes to release the essential oils from the spices.

2. Add the cubed lamb, mixing thoroughly with the spices, increase the temperature slightly to seal the meat and maintain the temperature at medium until the meat is sealed. Once this is done return the heat to low and place the lid on the pan. Cook for about 10 minutes on a low heat until the spices are infused and soaked into the meat. Now add the tomatoes and mix well. Cook without the lid for a further 5 minutes or until the oil separates from the mixture.

3. Once the acidity from the tomatoes has begun to break down, replace the lid and simmer for 20 minutes, occasionally stirring or shaking the pan to ensure that it's not sticking but don't be tempted to lift the lid off too frequently as the collection of steam is important to the cooking process. Add 300ml of hot water for half a kilo of lamb, or 400ml if you're cooking 1kg of lamb. Stir gently and continue cooking for a further 25-35 minutes or until the lamb is tender. If the mixture is too thick, add a little water to loosen to create more gravy. If it is too thin add a generous teaspoon of tomato puree.

4. Once cooked remove from the heat and leave to stand for a few minutes. Garnish with thin slices of ginger, coriander, a tiny sprinkle of garam masala and then a squeeze of fresh lemon juice.

Main Course Fish

The perception is that fish is not very well represented in Indian food but it couldn't be further away from the truth given the country's geography. India is surrounded by some of the best fishing waters in the Indian Ocean and Arabian Sea and enjoys a huge variety of fish and seafood. South Indian and Goan cuisine is particularly well known for its fish dishes.

I have very fond memories of visits to the fish market both in England and in India, two experiences that couldn't be more different to each other.

As a child I have vivid recollections of the long boats coming in and their nets spread out across the beach, selling directly to the locals and taking their catch to the local markets, and the intense smells of drying shrimp and mackerel with all the colours and smells being quite overwhelming. This was in stark contrast to local fish markets in Fleetwood on the Fylde in Lancashire, slightly cooler damper surroundings and somewhat more organized and orderly than my Indian experience!

Fish is cooked in many different ways in Indian cuisine and is often eaten as street food cooked dry on a tawa and served on a banana leaf. Fish is also often eaten in celebratory style on special days where speciality fish may be used.

In my experience people struggle to cook fish at the best of times. Whether it's a skill thing or whether it's the notion of eating fish per se, the strong smell and flavour of fish can often be a barrier.

At the cookery school my students often say they don't like the taste of 'fishy fish' such as salmon or mackerel!

In such cases I think the trick is to create a recipe that eliminates the fishy flavours and so the spices become the focus of the dish. There are a number of recipes in this chapter where I have achieved this to good effect and created dishes that are appealing to even those of you who might usually not enjoy the flavours of strong fish such as salmon.

Similarly, there are certain types of fish that are relatively bland and flavourless and so often are less appealing for their lack of discernible flavour, such as cod or haddock. This is where a spice blend or a simple well flavoured sauce can elevate the humble cod to a new and exciting level.

Makhan Raja Tiger Prawns

These creamy king prawns make for a refreshing mid-week change or it's a glorious dish to show off to your family and friends. It is a super speedy recipe to follow, despite the long list of ingredients. Prawns are a hugely underestimated source of protein, very low in fat and high in omega-3 fatty acids, so an all-round nutrient dense ingredient. Big on flavours, small on guilt!

Serves 4

Ingredients:

For the marinade:

600g raw king prawns – deveined and butterflied

4 tbsp. natural yoghurt

4 tbsp. double cream

2 tsp paprika

2 tsp tomato puree

½ tsp salt

2 tsp garlic

2 tsp ginger

2 tsp ground coriander

2 tsp ground cumin

3-finger pinches of fresh coriander

For the sauce:

3 tbsp. oil

2 tsp onion seeds

4 tsp garlic

300g tinned tomatoes

½ tsp salt

2 tsp ground cumin

2 tsp ground coriander

½ tsp garam masala

1 tsp finely chopped green chilli – or to taste

1 tsp jaggery

A dash of water

100ml double cream

3-finger pinches of fresh coriander to garnish

½ fresh lime for squeezing

1. Wash the prawns, drain them and squeeze out all of the water. Devein if not already done and butterfly the prawns to allow more flavour to soak into the prawn flesh.

2. In a separate bowl mix all the ingredients for the marinade (except the prawns), adjust to taste and add the prawns, mix well to coat them in the marinade and set aside in the fridge for an hour or two, time permitting.

3. When ready to cook, heat the oil in a pan, add the onion seeds and sizzle for a few seconds before adding the garlic and sauté for 15 seconds on a low heat before adding the tomatoes and then cook for 7-10 minutes on a low heat until the oil separates from the tomatoes.

4. Add the salt, cumin, ground coriander, garam masala, fresh green chilli and jaggery, and stir and cook on a low heat for a few minutes.

5. Now add the prawns and cook until they have just turned pink; it should only take 60-90 seconds or so. Add a dash of water, if required, to loosen the consistency.

6. Add the double cream and stir through gently, then remove from the heat.

7. Garnish with some fresh coriander and lime juice. Serve with crispy plain parathas or puri.

Kerala Fish Curry

South Indian curries are really quite different to the thicker sauces from northern India. This recipe is really simple and quick yet provides all the flavours you want, without a thick sauce as you might expect with meat dishes. Using shallots will make a big difference to the flavour as they will bring a sweet intensity. Do crush the fenugreek well to avoid a stringy, fibrous texture in the sauce.

Serves 4

Ingredients:
8 shallots – finely chopped
2 tbsp. oil
8 curry leaves
½ tsp freshly chopped green chilli
2 tsp chopped ginger
2 tsp chopped garlic
½ tsp hot chilli powder
½ tsp turmeric powder
2 tsp coriander powder
½ tsp crushed dried fenugreek leaves (crushed in a mortar and pestle)
Salt to taste
120ml warm water – or as required to create a little sauce/gravy
600g white fish – nothing too flaky; haddock or monkfish are ideal
Coriander for garnish

1. Start by finely chopping the shallots and set aside.

2. Heat the oil in a deep pan; add the curry leaves, shallots, green chilli, ginger and garlic and sauté for a few minutes.

3. Then add the chilli powder, turmeric, coriander powder, crushed fenugreek leaves and salt to taste and sauté again, mixing well to ensure that the dry spices are incorporated well.

4. Add water as required or to your preferred consistency.

5. When the sauce/gravy is simmering, add the fish pieces. Cook for a few minutes. When the fish is firm but tender, remove from the heat and garnish with coriander.

6. Serve immediately with saffron rice.

Meen Kulambu – Fish Curry

This dish is often served with idli, a steamed rice flour cake or even just plain steamed rice, as the tamarind sauce adds a delicious tangy flavour and the dish needs little else. Use fish such as pollock, hake or tilapia, as they tend to be less flaky when cooked.

Kulambu is also known as Kuzhambu. It is a gravy based on a broth made with tamarind and is typical of a south Indian fish dish originating from Kerala.

Serves 4

Ingredients:

For the paste:
1 small onion, chopped
1 small tomato
80g fresh or frozen coconut, grated or chopped
6 cloves of garlic, peeled
6 dried Kashmiri chillies, stalks snipped off (or medium hot dried red chillies)
1 tbsp. black peppercorns
1½ tsp salt

For the fish:
2 tbsp. oil
1 tsp black mustard seeds
1 tsp urid daal, husked (or black lentils)
6-8 curry leaves
1 tsp turmeric
150ml water
600g cod fillet (or pollock, haddock or hake) cut into 4cm chunks
Handful of coriander leaves for garnish

1. Put all the paste ingredients into a mini food processor and blend to a thick paste, adding a splash of water if needed.

2. Heat the oil in a heavy-based saucepan or karahi. Add the mustard seeds, and wait for them to finish popping before adding the urid daal and curry leaves, then add the paste and the turmeric and gently fry for 5 minutes until fragrant.

3. Add the water, bring to the boil and simmer for a few minutes before adding the fish. Cook for 4-5 minutes or until cooked through, very gently spooning some of the sauce over the fish, but avoid using a wide utensil as the fish is delicate and will break up.

4. Garnish by adding freshly chopped coriander to the pan and serve with rice or Indian bread.

Chilli Methi Prawns

I first tried a recipe similar to this at the Leela Palace hotel in Delhi. I sat for ages trying to decipher all the component parts; I made a note in my food journal and promptly re-created something similar back at home. I'm not sure it's exactly what I tasted but I perfected my version and have enjoyed sharing the dish with my family and friends ever since. The green spice paste could easily be used with any other fish to create a curry.

Serves 4

Ingredients:
20 large tail-on raw prawns

For the green spice paste:
½ tsp chopped green chillies
50g coriander leaves and stems
30g frozen peas, defrosted
2 tsp grated ginger
½ tsp salt
4 tsp lemon juice
1 tsp ground turmeric
1 tsp cumin seeds
1 tsp black peppercorns
1 tbsp. oil

3 tbsp. oil
½ medium onion, very finely chopped
2 tsp chopped garlic
1 tsp finely chopped ginger
1 tsp ground turmeric
½ tsp crushed coriander seeds
½ tsp red chilli flakes
½ tsp salt
1 bunch of fresh fenugreek leaves, stems removed, leaves finely chopped (or substitute 2 large handfuls of spinach – leaves very finely chopped)
1 tbsp. dried fenugreek leaves
2 tsp lemon juice
1 bunch of spring onions, green part only, very finely chopped
2 tbsp. coriander leaves – finely chopped
¼ tsp chaat masala

1. Peel, devein and butterfly the prawns leaving the tail attached. Rinse and pat dry.

2. Next prepare the green spice paste. Put all of the ingredients into a blender or mini processor and whizz to a fine paste. Spread half of the paste over the prawns and leave them to marinate in the fridge for 30 minutes.

3. Heat 2 tablespoons of the oil in a deep sauté pan. Add the remaining spice paste and cook gently for 2-3 minutes. Add the chopped onion and sauté over a very gentle heat until translucent. Add the garlic, ginger, turmeric, coriander seeds, chilli flakes, salt, fresh fenugreek leaves (or spinach if using), dried fenugreek leaves, lemon juice and spring onions. Cook, stirring occasionally for a further 10 minutes or until the fenugreek/spinach leaves have become very soft and all of the spices have been incorporated. Stir in the chopped coriander.

4. Heat the remaining 1 tablespoon of oil in a separate sauté pan and fry the marinated prawns for 1-2 minutes until they have just turned pink. Add the prawns to the onion mixture and simmer until cooked through.

5. Sprinkle with the chaat masala and serve immediately. The prawns are delicious when served on freshly cooked puri.

Prawn Masala Curry

This is a quick and easy dish yet pays amazing dividends in flavour. It can be thrown together in less time than it takes to butterfly the prawns, which is essential so that they soak up all the flavours in the sauce. This is delicious served with naan bread to mop up all the fragrant flavours.

Serves 4

Ingredients:
600g uncooked tiger prawns –
deveined and butterflied
3 tbsp. oil
1 star anise
1 tsp onion seeds
4 tsp finely chopped garlic
4 tsp finely chopped ginger
300g chopped tomatoes – tinned
½ tsp hot chilli powder
1 tsp turmeric
1 tsp salt, or to taste
2 tsp ground cumin
2 tsp ground coriander
2 x 3-finger pinch fresh coriander
for cooking and garnish
100ml hot water or to desired
consistency
Squeeze of lemon to finish

1. Gently heat the oil in a deep pan on a low heat. Add the star anise and onion seeds, and sizzle for a few seconds before adding the garlic and ginger; cook on a low heat for 2 minutes.

2. Add the tomatoes, turn up the heat to medium, stir in and once the temperature is back to simmer, turn down the heat to low once again and cook for a further 8-10 minutes. Once the tomatoes begin to coagulate and you have eliminated the water from the tomatoes, add the chilli powder, turmeric, salt, cumin, ground coriander and fresh coriander – stir well to ensure they are thoroughly integrated and cook on a gentle heat for 5 minutes.

3. Add the prawns and 100ml of boiling water and mix well to ensure all the spices have coated the prawns.

4. On a medium heat, cook with the lid on for just a few minutes or until the prawns have turned pink.

5. Remove from the heat, garnish with lemon juice and remaining coriander and serve immediately with naan bread, hot chapattis or roti and rice.

Chef's Tips:

1. Substitute the prawns for tofu, paneer or any other vegetables if desired.

2. Add some finely chopped spinach at the end of the cooking process to increase the nutrient value, making it close to a methi prawn dish.

Cod in Tamarind Sauce

This recipe is the equivalent of using soy sauce and honey in Chinese or Japanese cuisine. I adore the sticky tar-like onion consistency that almost sticks to the fork like a gooey BBQ sauce. The onion with the sauce adds a lovely texture to the dish to complement the fish (though I also use tofu on occasions). I recommend using a firm white fish, although it works with salmon too. Cod steaks are a good idea though they can be difficult to find in the local supermarket since most fish is filleted these days. A good local fishmonger would be able to help.

Serves 4

Ingredients:

For the fish marinade:
2 tbsp. oil
1 tsp wholegrain mustard
1 tsp turmeric
2 tsp finely chopped garlic
¼ tsp salt
½ tsp black pepper
2 tbsp. finely chopped fresh coriander
Salt to taste
4 pieces of cod steak or fillets (haddock or other white fish is fine)

3 tbsp. oil
1 medium onion finely chopped
1 tsp garlic
2 tbsp. of tamarind pulp or tamarind sauce (see recipe in sauces and salads chapter)
1 tsp sugar (if using tamarind pulp rather than sauce)
Fresh coriander to garnish
Lemon juice to garnish

1. Place all the ingredients for the marinade in a bowl, mix and taste to adjust the seasoning if required. Add the fish and coat evenly. Set aside.

2. Now heat the oil in a wide pan, add the onion and garlic and cook for a few minutes on a gentle heat until the onion has softened.

3. Add the tamarind sauce or pulp (if you are using unsweetened pulp then add the sugar as well). Stir the tamarind into the onions and cook for 1-2 minutes.

4. Place the fish, skin side up (if not using cod steak), into the pan, spooning over any leftover marinade from the bowl. Spoon some of the onion and tamarind sauce over the fish.

5. Cook the fish for about 5 minutes on the first side on a low heat. Check the colour of the fish to see whether the flesh has turned white and if so turn the fish over.

6. Cook with the skin side down for a further minute or two before switching off and let it rest in the pan for a minute before serving up. Garnish with fresh coriander and lemon juice.

Halibut with Fenugreek Leaves

This is a very simple fish curry, knocked out in minutes, and usually accompanies an equally simple lentil dish. A great winter warmer and protein rich supper that could equally be eaten on its own or with a hot wholemeal flour roti to mop up the sauce.

Serves 4

Ingredients:
3 tbsp. oil
1 tsp onion seeds
2 tbsp. gram flour
150g tinned tomatoes or passata
2 tsp finely chopped garlic
½ tsp hot chilli powder
½ tsp turmeric
1 tsp ground cumin
1 tsp ground coriander
1 tbsp. dried fenugreek leaves
¼ tsp salt or to taste
150ml of hot water or to preference
500g halibut or haddock or any firm white fish
Full hand pinch of fresh coriander for garnish
A squeeze of lemon juice for garnish

1. Heat the oil in a wide, heavy pan, add the onion seeds and sizzle for a few seconds before adding the gram flour. Stir and ensure that there is enough oil to cook out the flour before adding the tomatoes. Stir and cook for a few minutes until the oil begins to separate.

2. Now add the garlic and chilli powder, turmeric, cumin, ground coriander, dried fenugreek leaves and salt, and stir and cook for a further minute, to allow the spices to meld into the tomato base. Taste to adjust the seasoning as necessary.

3. Add the water and stir it into the sauce base, incorporating all the spices.

4. Now add the fish and spoon the sauce over the fish; stir very gently to ensure you don't break up the fish, but ensure that the fish is evenly coated in the spices.

5. Place the lid on the pan and cook for 4-5 minutes or until the fish is cooked. Taste again to adjust the seasoning if necessary.

6. Remove from the heat and garnish with fresh coriander and lemon juice.

7. Serve immediately.

Chef's Tip:

Use frozen fish to save time and use as a quick unplanned dinner. Frozen fish is extremely useful, sustainable and fresh as the freshness is locked in.

Monkfish in Curry Leaves

This recipe is a jewel amongst my seafood repertoire, not least because I'm using monkfish. It is the citrus flavour of the lemon juice and zest that makes this dish stand out from the crowd. I was inspired to create this recipe after a visit to Fort Aguada in Goa where the chef in a garden restaurant we were visiting insisted I try his special fish dish. Although the flavours were sensational, it got me thinking about what fish I would use if I were to do my own take on this recipe.

Serves 4

Ingredients:

For the marinade:
3 tbsp. oil
½ tsp red chilli powder
¼ tsp turmeric
1 tsp ground fennel seeds
Juice and zest of 1 lemon
1 tsp jaggery
½ tsp salt or to taste

For the fish:
600g monkfish
3 tbsp. oil

For the sauce:
3 tbsp. oil
1 star anise
1 tsp onion seeds
12 curry leaves
2 medium onions – finely sliced
2 tsp finely chopped ginger
¼ tsp turmeric
¼ tsp chilli powder
½ tsp ground fennel
3-finger pinch fresh coriander
½ tsp salt
1 tsp jaggery
1½ tbsp. lemon juice
150ml water
1 large handful fresh coriander
leaves to garnish

1. Combine the ingredients for the marinade in a bowl. Mix well and rub the marinade into the monkfish. Set aside for 30 minutes in a cool place.

2. Heat the oil in a large pan, add the monkfish and fry for about 1 minute on each side until lightly coloured. Remove the fish onto a plate and set aside. To make the sauce, add the additional oil to the pan, gently heat the oil before adding the star anise, onion seeds and curry leaves, allow to infuse for a few seconds.

3. Now add the sliced onions and sauté on a low heat until the onions have softened and are lightly brown in colour.

4. Lower the heat and add the ginger, turmeric, chilli powder, ground fennel, fresh coriander, salt, jaggery and lemon juice. Stir well and cook for 1 minute before adding 150ml of water.

5. Bring to the boil and simmer for a few minutes, allowing all the spices to integrate together. Return the monkfish, juices, and remaining marinade to the pan and stir gently.

6. Cover with a lid and cook for 7-10 minutes until the fish is tender, checking halfway through and spooning some of the liquid over the fish. Remove from the heat and place on a serving dish. Garnish with fresh coriander leaves.

Chef's Tip:

If you're making this dish for guests and want to plan ahead then take the dish up to the point where you bring the sauce up to a simmer, switch off, and let the sauce develop over a few hours. Then bring to the boil and add the fish when you are ready to serve.

Roasted Sea Bass with Red Peppers & Olives

Olives? I totally agree that they're not Indian but they add a great flavour all the same and I am unashamedly experimental, and if I find something I like, I am going use it, no matter which continent it belongs to.

Serves 4

Ingredients:
1 tbsp. oil
1 tsp garlic
1 tbsp. green olives – finely chopped
¼ tsp chilli, red or green, or ½ bullet chilli
1 tbsp. fresh coriander, finely chopped – keep back a little to garnish
100g chopped tinned tomatoes
⅛ tsp salt
⅛ tsp black pepper or to taste
1 tsp paprika
1 tsp jaggery or honey
¼ red pepper very finely cubed

2 fillets of sea bass or similar white fish

1. In a medium frying pan, heat the oil; add the garlic, olives, chilli, and fresh coriander. Stir well and cook for 1-2 minutes on a low heat, then add the tomatoes, stir again and bring up to a simmer. (Use fresh plum tomatoes from the garden when in season but otherwise tinned plum tomatoes are fine.)

2. Simmer for 5 minutes on a medium to low heat until the tomatoes start to coagulate. Now add the salt, pepper, paprika and jaggery or honey.

3. Once the oil begins to separate from the tomatoes and the acidity is lost, add ¾ of the finely cubed pepper (save a little for garnishing on top). Switch off the heat.

4. When the mixture has cooled completely, place one of the fillets, skin side up, on a baking tray, and spread the tomato filling over the fillet generously. Now lay the second fillet with the skin side on top, and brush the top of the fish with a little of the oil from the pan. Scatter the remaining red peppers over the top. Bake in the oven for 12 minutes at 170°C/gas mark 5.

5. Rest the fish for 2 minutes before serving. Garnish with the remaining fresh chopped coriander. Serve with a potato dish and salad.

Goan Salmon Infused in a Garlic & Black Pepper Spice Blend

This is the dish that has converted the most non-fish eaters on our cookery classes. Salmon is often known for being fishy or just plain boring, cooked with a bit of lemon and pepper. And so this simple marinade utterly transforms this ubiquitous fish into a flavour sensation.

Serves 4

For the marinade:
2 tbsp. oil
2 tbsp. lemon juice – or you can use bottled lemon juice
2 tsp chopped garlic
1 tsp ground cumin
1 tsp ground coriander
¼ tsp black pepper
¼ tsp salt
⅛ tsp hot red chilli powder
¼ tsp turmeric
2 x 3-finger pinch fresh coriander, finely chopped

4 pieces of salmon fillet

For the garnish:
Fresh coriander, finely chopped
Slices of fresh apple, julienned

1. Place all the ingredients for the marinade in a big bowl and taste.

2. Add the fish and set aside to marinate for 30 minutes or so.

3. Place the salmon on a tray under a hot grill about 3 inches away from the heat for approximately 10-12 minutes or place in a preheated oven for 15 minutes at 170°C.

4. Garnish with chopped fresh coriander and julienne of apple. Alternatively, for restaurant style presentation garnish with amarynth, micro coriander and julienne of apple!

Chef's Tips:

1. *To make a spice blend for long shelf life (refrigerates for up to 3 months), leave out the fresh coriander and replace the freshly squeezed lemon juice for bottled. This can now be stored in a sterilized glass jar in the fridge and used in the same way as pesto or a marinade sauce. This spice blend is suitable for freezing for longer shelf life.*

2. *This spice blend is also great with chicken which can be roasted, grilled or pan-fried just like the fish.*

Vegetables & Sides

Having grown up in a largely vegetarian household, vegetable dishes have always played a major role at the table. In Indian cuisine vegetables and lentils are never relegated to the role of sides but are very much a main part of the daily and weekly repertoire. Whilst this may not be your experience of Indian restaurants, remember they have tried to give customers what they think they want, believing the meat is always central to the table.

The notion of eating meat or fish at every meal is certainly not the case in an average Indian household. I'd be inclined to say that meat or fish is rarely served more than three times a week, not because meat is seen as a luxury item, but rather that meat and fish are not the only source of protein and in order to have a balance of vitamins and minerals from a varied source, eating a broader range of vegetables and lentils will keep the nutrients balance happy as well as the taste buds.

Eating seasonally is also important and so I am inclined to wait for my favourite vegetables to be in season. I think it's fair to say that nature plans for perfection, so if we follow the natural cycle and eat seasonal foods, we will optimize the nutritional value when we most need those particular nutrients and therefore we can be healthier in readiness for each season. So my motto is to buy what is available in abundance to eat and enjoy it at its freshest.

Having grown up in a fairly rural landscape I have great memories of pulling vegetables from the earth, rich and muddy and totally organic. As a child I was pained to peel such muddy potatoes and carrots and dirty Brussels sprouts but I still remember the flavours to this day. Thus I have a strong affinity with the concept of eating locally grown vegetables having enjoyed their earthy sweetness, whether it was potatoes in Lancashire or okra from Gujarat. It's a powerful recollection that resonates with me and so even today I look for the natural flavours of food; it's in my heart and soul.

Historically speaking much of India has been vegetarian, though this statistic has changed dramatically over the last 50 years with only 30% of the population still practising a vegetarian lifestyle, and so vegetables have always been the main dish for most and never just a sideshow. In fact if you were trying to practise a more vegetarian lifestyle, then Indian food offers the greatest variety of vegetables and recipes.

For me, any dish, vegetables or otherwise, has to have the 'wow factor' and so the dishes I have included in this chapter are definitely worthy of being the main characters on the stage. I have tried to use ingredients that will be readily available to ensure you have the opportunity to try all the recipes.

Green Beans with Cashew Nuts

If ever I'm feeling the need to be super healthy I'll make this dish for dinner and enjoy it with nothing else. Green beans are an excellent source of protein, iron, calcium, magnesium, vitamin B6, fibre and vitamin K. The dish itself is very light and the crunchy texture from the cashew nuts is quite delicious. I regularly make this dish when entertaining because it's easy, unusual and very well received by all.

Serves 4 as a side dish

Ingredients:
300g fine green beans trimmed – cut into half
1½ tbsp. oil
1 tsp yellow mustard seeds
8 curry leaves
2 tsp finely chopped garlic
2 tsp finely chopped ginger
½ medium mild chilli cut into thin julienne strips
½ tsp turmeric
½ tsp salt
3 tbsp. hot water
2 tbsp. cashew nuts

To finish:
Handful of coconut flakes – toasted
Crispy pre-fried onions to garnish

1. Wash and trim the green beans, drain in a colander and set aside.

2. In a wide sauté pan (with a lid) heat the oil, add the mustard seeds and wait until they finish popping before adding the curry leaves followed by the garlic and ginger. Cook for 2-3 minutes on a gentle heat.

3. Now add the chilli, turmeric and salt. Cook the spices on a low heat for 1-2 minutes.

4. Add the green beans, stir the spices into the beans and cook without the lid for a minute.

5. Add the hot water and then place the lid on and cook for 10 minutes on a low heat, stirring occasionally.

6. Meanwhile roast the cashew nuts in the oven until they are lightly browned and set aside. Separately toast the coconut flakes until they are very lightly brown; be careful as they can brown very quickly.

7. When the beans are ready throw in the cashew nuts and stir through.

8. Turn out onto the serving dish and scatter over the toasted coconut flakes and pre-fried onions.

9. Serve immediately.

Pau Bhaji

Though this dish originates from Mumbai, pau bhaji is a well-loved dish all over India. Pau means 'a small bun', while bhaji means 'vegetables'. The wholesomeness of this dish lends itself to being a meal in its own right as well as a hot favourite Indian street food. Scores of vendors can be seen in streets all over Mumbai where it is probably most popular, energetically stirring up its ingredients on huge sizzling pans. The recipe for the pau bhaji masala spice blend can be found on page 315.

Serves 4

Ingredients:
2 tbsp. oil
50g butter, cubed
2 tsp cumin seeds
2 medium onions, finely chopped
½ red capsicum
½ green capsicum
2 large tomatoes – or several baby plum tomatoes, chopped finely
2 tsp ginger
1 tsp green chilli
4 tbsp. pau bhaji spice blend
1 tsp salt
2 tbsp. tomato puree
200g cooked potatoes, roughly mashed – something like Maris Pipers
200g cooked cauliflower, roughly mashed
200g cooked aubergine, roughly mashed
300ml water held back from the boiled vegetables
30g garden peas
2 tbsp. lemon juice or ⅛ segment of fresh lemon
2 tbsp. finely chopped fresh coriander

4 soft rolls
Butter to griddle the rolls

1. In a deep or wok-like pan add the oil and butter – heat gently and add the cumin seeds. Sizzle for a few seconds before adding the onions. Cook for 5 minutes until the onions are soft and losing their texture then add the capsicum.

2. Now add the tomatoes, ginger and chilli and stir them into the onions. Cook for 7-8 minutes on a low heat to a soft pulp.

3. Add the spice blend, salt and tomato puree to the pan and stir well, cook for a few minutes to allow the flavours to blend together before adding the potatoes, cauliflower and aubergine. Add 150ml of water and then add a little water, bit by bit, until the desired consistency is achieved.

4. Cook for about 5 minutes to allow all the flavours and ingredients to acquaint themselves in the pan. Add the peas and stir in.

5. Add the lemon juice – stir in followed by the fresh coriander.

6. Now prepare the 'pau' – slice the bread buns (regular soft rolls) in half through the middle as if preparing a sandwich. Heat a griddle or frying pan and melt a knob of butter. Once melted place the bread buns in the butter (the inside of the bread roll) and toast in the pan until crispy and golden brown. Turn over and press the bread down for just a few seconds before removing. Place on the side of the serving plate and then serve your portion of bhaji over one side of the bread – almost like beans on toast.

Chef's Tips:

1. *Put the potatoes, cauliflower and aubergine together and cook in the pressure cooker for speed and energy efficiency.*

2. *You can use tinned tomatoes but I find baby plum tomatoes add more flavour. Better still if they come straight from the garden in season!*

Baby Turnips in Chickpea Masala

Baby turnips are native to Western Asia and have been used in Indian cookery for many years; they are favoured for their peppery flavour, similar to arugula (rocket). Baby turnips are available locally when in season, which is June or July in the UK. This is not necessarily the time that you want to eat a root vegetable but they are delicious as a side dish or even mashed.

Serves 4 as a side dish

Ingredients:
6 fresh baby plum tomatoes, deseeded and chopped finely
10 baby turnips, washed, trimmed and cut into quarters
2 tbsp. oil
1 tsp brown mustard seeds
1 tsp cumin seeds
¼ tsp asafoetida

Chickpea flour masala mix:
4 tbsp. gram flour
2 tbsp. oil
1 tsp turmeric
1 tsp ground coriander seeds
1 tsp salt
¼ tsp baking powder
1 tsp ground cumin seeds
¼ tsp chilli powder

150ml water
2 green spring onions sliced diagonally
Juice of half a lemon

Freshly chopped coriander to garnish

1. Deseed and finely chop the tomatoes.

2. Parboil or steam the turnips until they are about 60% cooked. Refresh in cold water and set aside. In a bowl bring together all the ingredients for the chickpea masala. Gently massage the ingredients into each other until they resemble fine breadcrumbs or just becoming a roux.

3. Heat 2 tablespoons of oil in a large non-stick pan and add the mustard seeds. Once they have popped, add the cumin seeds, asafoetida and tomatoes. Cook for 2-3 minutes on a low heat until the tomatoes have become soft.

4. Add the turnips, stir well and cook for 2-3 minutes on a low heat. Now add the chickpea masala and stir gently, then cook for about a minute before adding the water.

5. Bring up to a simmer and cook for 5 minutes until the turnips are cooked through. Add the sliced spring onions. Add the lemon juice and stir thoroughly. Garnish with freshly chopped coriander.

6. Serve with hot buttery chapattis.

Spicy Aubergine Fingers with Fennel

This is a lovely warming dish in which the aubergines soak up all of the flavours of the spices, bringing an amazing depth of flavour to every mouthful. The fennel seeds add a delicious aniseedy touch to round things off. Aubergines are underrated, but when cooked properly they have an almost meaty texture and are a great source of copper, magnesium and potassium and are also rich in antioxidants.

Serves 4

Ingredients:
500g baby aubergines cut into wedges 4-5cm long
Oil for brushing aubergines
2 tbsp. oil
1 tsp onion seeds
1 tsp mustard seeds
1 tsp fennel seeds
3 tsp garlic (3 cloves, minced)
2 tsp grated ginger
200g tinned chopped tomatoes
2 tsp ground coriander
2 tsp ground cumin
½ tsp turmeric
½ tsp chilli powder
½ tsp cinnamon powder
1 tsp salt
1 tbsp. freshly chopped coriander + 1 tbsp. to garnish
Freshly grated coconut (optional)

1. Preheat the oven to 180°C/gas mark 4.

2. Wash and dry the aubergines whilst whole then quarter them lengthways. Brush lightly with oil and place on a roasting tray in the oven for 25 minutes.

3. Heat 2 tablespoons of oil in a pan and add the onion seeds, mustard seeds and fennel seeds. Sizzle for a few seconds and then add the garlic and ginger and sauté for 2 minutes before adding the chopped tomatoes. Cook for 5-7 minutes on a low heat until the oil starts to separate and the tomatoes coagulate.

4. Now add the ground coriander, ground cumin, turmeric, chilli powder, cinnamon, salt and fresh coriander and cook for a few minutes on a low heat to avoid burning them.

5. Carefully add the cooked aubergine; stir well but gently so as not to break the aubergines. Cover the pan with a tight fitting lid and cook for about 10 minutes on a low heat.

6. Garnish with fresh coriander and fresh grated coconut if you have some, but frozen grated coconut is also fine.

7. Enjoy with parathas or rotis.

The Original Bombay Potatoes

I've always called this recipe 'The Original Bombay Potatoes' as this distinguishes it from the tomato-based potato curry often served in restaurants as 'Bombay potatoes' when in fact this is a recipe also known as 'aloo dum'. My authentic version is always a hit in my cookery classes as it's fresh, delicious and super easy to make. For a dish with so few ingredients the flavour profile is simply sensational and it's great served alongside most curries, or even eaten cold as a salad.

Serves 4

Ingredients:
750g small new potatoes, boiled
2 tbsp. rapeseed oil
1 tsp whole black mustard seeds
¼ tsp asafoetida
3 heaped tsp chopped garlic
½ tsp salt or to taste
¼ tsp finely chopped green chilli or
½ tsp ground black pepper
1 tsp turmeric
2 x 1 tbsp. fresh coriander – finely chopped
3 stalks of spring onion (green part only), sliced thinly diagonally (optional)

1. Scrub the potatoes and cut them into quarters where they are larger so that you have about ½ inch round pieces. Place them in a pan covered with cold water and 1 teaspoon of salt. Boil until they are cooked through. Drain in a colander and set aside.

2. Now heat the oil in a pan, and when the oil is hot but not smoking add the mustard seeds. Keep a lid to hand and cover the pan until the seeds stop popping.

3. Once the seeds have popped add the asafoetida, garlic, salt, chilli and turmeric, and cook until it sizzles then immediately add the potatoes and stir.

4. Add half of the fresh coriander and stir through once again. Make sure all of the spices are mixed into the potatoes and continue to cook for a few minutes until the potatoes are hot and crunchy at the sides.

5. Remove from the heat, garnish with the remaining coriander and serve. Scatter over the spring onions (if using).

Chef's Tip:

You could add 100g of fresh baby spinach, finely chopped, a minute before taking off the heat; just allow the spinach to wilt and move around the pan so that it wilts evenly. This will give you a fresh version of 'saag aloo'.

Palak Paneer

This recipe is a firm favourite with my daughter Savannah who loves paneer in any form. I insist that it's made with fresh baby spinach leaves. It takes minutes to blanch and then it's thrown into a food processor. It diminishes into nothing and then magically reappears in volume in the cooking process. This is another firm favourite when entertaining; your guests will notice the difference between the restaurant version and yours for sure.

Serves 4 as a side dish

Ingredients:
200g baby spinach – blanched in slightly salted hot water, cooled and blended into a puree.
2 tbsp. + 1 tbsp. oil
100g paneer – cut into cubes
1 cinnamon stick
1 tsp cumin seeds
1 medium onion – finely chopped
1 tsp finely chopped ginger
1 tsp finely chopped garlic
50g tinned tomato, chopped
¼ tsp hot chilli powder
1 tsp ground cumin
1 tsp ground coriander
¼ tsp garam masala
½ tsp Himalayan salt
1 tbsp. finely chopped fresh coriander + 1 tbsp. finely chopped fresh coriander (for garnishing)
1 tbsp. single cream and a knob of butter for garnish

1. Plunge the spinach into a pan of hot salted water for 1 minute. Drain thoroughly and squeeze out any excess water. Place into a food processor and blitz until pureed. Set aside.

2. Heat 2 tablespoons of oil on a low heat in a medium saucepan; add the paneer and lightly fry to achieve a pale golden colour. When it has been evenly coloured, remove from the pan and set aside.

3. Add another 1 tablespoon of oil to the pan, and when the oil is hot add the cinnamon stick and sizzle for a few seconds before adding the cumin seeds, followed by the onion. Cook the onion on a low heat until it is soft and translucent.

4. Add ginger and garlic and cook on a low heat for 2 minutes.

5. Add the tomato, stir well and continue to cook on a low heat until the oil begins to separate from the tomatoes. This should take about 5 minutes or so, though if you are using fresh tomatoes this could take a little longer.

6. Add all the dry spices: chilli, ground cumin, coriander, garam masala, salt, and 1 tablespoon of chopped coriander, and cook for 5 minutes on a low heat to cook the spices.

7. Now add the spinach puree and paneer. Stir the ingredients into the spices and cook on a low heat with the lid on for 5 minutes. Add a little water to loosen the consistency if necessary.

8. Finally add the butter, cream and a final pinch of fresh coriander to garnish before serving, and serve hot.

Cauliflower & Potatoes (Aloo Gobi)

I grew up eating this dish and always referred to it as the dish with the little trees in it. When it was my job to prepare the cauliflower, I would diligently cut them to ensure the 'trees' were still in their perfect form.

Cauliflower is a powerhouse of vitamin C: just 100g will provide 80% of your recommended daily allowance. It's a no-brainer!

Serves 6-8 as a side dish

Ingredients:
1 cauliflower cut into individual small florets (trees!) and washed
300g baby new potatoes – peeled and boiled
30ml oil
1 tsp cumin seeds
10 curry leaves (optional)
200g pureed tinned tomatoes
2 tsp finely chopped ginger
½ tsp turmeric
1½ tsp salt or to taste
¾ tsp red chilli powder
1 tsp ground cumin
1 tsp ground coriander
1½ tbsp. fresh coriander
Pinch of garam masala to garnish

1. Steam the cauliflower to almost about 80% cooked, and boil or steam the potatoes to 95% cooked.

2. Heat the oil in a pan, add the cumin seeds and the curry leaves and then add the tomatoes. Cook on a medium heat to cook off the acidity and water in the tomatoes.

3. Add the ginger and allow it to sauté for a minute before adding the rest of the spices: turmeric, salt, chilli powder, cumin and ground coriander. Allow the spices to blend together for a minute or two before adding the cauliflower and potatoes; mix well.

4. Cook for 5 minutes on a low heat with the lid on. When the cauliflower and potato are cooked through, add the fresh coriander and garam masala to garnish and serve.

Spinach and Beetroot with Roasted Coriander Seeds

This is a recipe I created in almost laboratory style conditions as part of my dissertation research whilst studying food science. I wanted to bring together a variety of ingredients to create an ultra-healthy Indian recipe to cook by numbers. The result is a dish in which the flavours are light and uncomplicated and aptly demonstrate the numerous superfoods used in Indian cuisine.

Serves 4

Ingredients:
2 tsp coriander seeds – roughly milled
1 dried red chilli
30g or 2 tbsp. red skinned peanuts roasted and roughly chopped
1 tbsp. oil
2 tsp garlic
1 medium finely chopped onion
½ tsp turmeric
½ to ¾ tsp salt
4 baby plum tomatoes cut lengthways.
50g beetroot cut into julienne strips
250g baby/young spinach leaves

1. Lightly roast the coriander seeds and the whole chilli for a few minutes either in a wok or in an oven. Crush them in a pestle and mortar and then set aside.

2. Roast the red skinned peanuts separately and when cooled crush them a little and discard the excess skin shells; set them aside.

3. Heat the oil in a deep pan or wok and add the crushed chilli and coriander. Sizzle for 30 seconds or until you smell a gentle aroma.

4. Add the chopped garlic and onion and cook for approximately 5 to 6 minutes until lightly golden brown. Now add the turmeric, salt and tomatoes, and stir in to blend the colours.

5. Follow with the beetroot and then a minute later the spinach.

6. Gently fold the spinach into the onion and spice mixture. Turn the spinach over to take heat from the base of the pan, but be careful not to overcook it or allow the moisture to release from the spinach.

7. Just as the spinach is beginning to wilt, remove from the heat and sprinkle on the peanuts. Toss gently and serve immediately with some chapattis or potatoes.

Dry Stuffed Okra

People tend to avoid okra for its perceived slimy texture, which only becomes so if the sap inside the okra is exposed to moisture before it has cooked through. However this is an extremely nutritious vegetable known for its cancer fighting and iron-rich properties. As an added bonus this dish is utterly delicious and the stuffing can be used for many other vegetables too.

Serves 4

Ingredients:
20 okras – washed, dried whole and tops trimmed off
4 tbsp. oil
150g gram flour
3 tsp garlic, finely chopped
3 tsp ginger, finely chopped
1 tsp green chilli, finely chopped
½ tsp of salt or to taste
1 tsp turmeric
1 tbsp. lemon juice
2 tbsp. fresh coriander
2 tbsp. crushed peanut powder
1 tsp sesame seeds
1 tsp Kashmiri chilli powder

For the tarka:
2 tbsp. oil
1 tsp cumin seeds
¼ tsp asafoetida
10 curry leaves

Fresh coriander to garnish
Crushed peanuts to garnish

1. Wash the okra and, using a clean cloth, towel dry each one individually. Set aside on a fresh, dry cloth for a few hours in an ambient temperature for the okra to dry.

2. Meanwhile, gently heat the oil in a pan, add the gram flour and cook on a low heat, stirring constantly to ensure it doesn't burn. When golden brown, remove from the heat.

3. Add the garlic, ginger, green chilli, salt, turmeric, lemon juice, fresh coriander, crushed peanut powder, sesame seeds and Kashmiri chilli powder to the flour. Stir the mixture well until all of the ingredients are combined. Set aside to cool down.

4. When the okra is dry make an incision down the middle and stuff with the filling, ensuring that you fill to the ends of the okra.

5. To make the tarka infusion, gently heat the oil in a wide-based pan, add the cumin seeds, asafoetida and curry leaves and sizzle for a few seconds before adding the okra and any remaining stuffing mixture to the pan. Cook on a low heat with a cover on the pan. Stir occasionally to ensure that it doesn't stick, adding some oil if necessary; allow any condensation from the pan lid to fall in to create a steaming effect.

6. When the okra is cooked, remove it from the heat, garnish with fresh coriander and a sprinkling of crushed peanuts and serve immediately.

Cabbage and Turmeric Stir-Fry

With its origins deep in the heart of Kerala this is essentially a stir-fried light vegetable dish. In Kerala it might be made with ingredients such as snake beans and green tomatoes however the point is that one should use common ingredients because it is a simple everyday dish. Turmeric is a powerful ingredient with many health yielding properties; cooked with simplicity those nutritional values will yield great benefit to one's wellbeing. This recipe is a perfect illustration of how highly nutritional ingredients are woven into the daily diet in Indian cuisine.

Serves 4

Ingredients:
3 tbsp. oil
2 tbsp. black mustard seeds
¼ tsp asafoetida
10 curry leaves
50g fresh turmeric, sliced into julienne strips
2 green chillies sliced into julienne strips
2 tsp ginger, finely grated into a paste
½ tsp salt
250g cabbage (or spring greens), shredded into 5mm pieces
Fresh coriander to garnish

1. Heat the oil in a heavy-based saucepan or karahi set over a medium heat and when it is hot add the mustard seeds. Allow the mustard seeds to pop, and when they have finished popping add the asafoetida followed by the curry leaves.

2. Stir for about 10 seconds, before adding the fresh turmeric, fresh chillies, ginger paste and salt and stir-fry for 15 seconds.

3. Stir in the cabbage making sure the cabbage is fully coated with all of the spices and cook, covered, over a medium heat for 5-7 minutes or until the cabbage is tender, adding a splash of water if they start to stick to the pan.

4. Garnish with the fresh coriander.

Ginger Roasted Potatoes with Red Skinned Peanuts & Lime

This recipe was a firm favourite at The Saffron House, the original catering arm of The Cooking Academy, a real crowd pleaser with simplicity being the essence of the dish. Just the right amount of heat, salt and lime juice with traces of the curry leaves running through it, finished off with the roasted peanuts for bags of texture – perfect!

Serves 4

Ingredients:

750g Maris Piper potatoes – peeled and boiled in salted water until cooked but still firm, cut into 1 inch cubes

½ tsp chilli flakes

¼ tsp salt

2 tbsp. roughly chopped roasted red skinned peanuts (1 tbsp. + 1 tbsp.)

1 tsp dry urid lentils (white lentils)

2 tbsp. oil

2 tsp cumin seeds

¼ tsp asafoetida

Handful of curry leaves

2 tsp grated ginger

½ tsp chaat masala

1 tbsp. freshly chopped coriander

Juice of a lime or lemon

1. Whilst the potatoes are cold add them to a bowl with the chilli flakes, salt and a few of the peanuts. Gently toss them together without breaking up the potato.

2. Heat the pan you will be using to cook and dry fry the urid lentils for a minute on a gentle heat. Remove and set aside.

3. Heat the oil in a pan, and add the cumin seeds followed by the asafoetida, roasted urid lentils and curry leaves. Sizzle for a few seconds before adding the ginger, and cook for a minute before adding the seasoned potatoes.

4. Heat gently until all the spices have cooked in.

5. Turn off the heat, garnish with a few more of the peanuts, chaat masala, coriander and lime or lemon juice.

6. Serve immediately!

Chef's Tip:

You may need a little more oil – perhaps 2 tbsp. but try with 1 tbsp. first and add more later if required. This may depend on the type of potato and the level of firmness; the softer the potato the more oil it will absorb.

Pan-Fried Paneer in a Cashew Nut Sauce

The inclusion of cashew nuts is a means of eliminating onions that are often relied upon to make a sauce. Instead the use of nuts is a simple way of increasing the protein content of this dish whilst providing a rich and creamy consistency without the cream. Vegetarians beware, it will be difficult to keep the meat eaters away from this exotic and mouth-watering curry as in my experience it has universal appeal.

Serves 4

Ingredients:
3 tbsp. oil
300g paneer
25g or a generous knob of butter
2 cinnamon sticks
1 tsp onion seeds
2 tsp garlic, finely chopped
2 tsp ginger, finely chopped
400g passata or chopped tinned tomatoes
1 tsp paprika
1 tsp ground cumin
½ tsp turmeric
1 tsp ground cinnamon powder
1 tsp hot red chilli powder
1 tsp jaggery
1 tsp salt or to taste
100g ground cashew nuts
100g fresh garden peas
1 red bell chilli/capsicum cut 1 cm square
200ml hot water
Garam masala to garnish
2 tbsp. fresh chopped coriander (1 x spices + 1 x garnish)

1. Heat 3 tablespoons of oil in a pan on a low heat and gently shallow fry the paneer until it is lightly brown and a little crispy at the edges; you're just trying to seal it and give it a bit of crispy texture and colour. Set aside.

2. Now heat the butter in the remaining oil and add the cinnamon sticks and the onion seeds, followed by the garlic and ginger. Cook for 3 minutes and then add the tomatoes. Stir into the garlic and ginger, and cook for 10-12 minutes on a low heat to cook out the acidity and to allow the water from the tomatoes to evaporate. Whilst the tomatoes are cooking out gather the paprika, cumin, turmeric, cinnamon powder, chilli powder, jaggery and salt in a cup.

3. When the tomatoes are ready and you see a little oil separation, add the cup of spices and the ground cashew nuts. Stir well and keep cooking for about 5 minutes on a low heat to ensure that the spices don't burn.

4. Return the paneer to the pan and add the peas and capsicum. Stir in and allow them soak into the spices and the sauce.

5. Now add 200ml hot water or to your preference to achieve the viscosity you prefer. Cook for 5 minutes to allow the water to blend into the sauce.

6. Turn off the heat. Garnish with garam masala and fresh coriander.

7. Serve with parathas or fresh chapatti.

Chef's Tip:

You could also use this recipe for chicken, however marinate the chicken first in a simple spice blend, then stir-fry to seal the chicken first.

Green Banana & Peanut Curry

Green bananas are not usually associated with Indian cuisine however they have become more widely used in Gujarati cooking as a result of the migration from India to East Africa, in particular Kenya and Uganda, and have subsequently made their way over to the UK. This dish is absolute proof that we live in a global village and since green bananas are readily available, I would highly recommend you ring the changes and try this curry out. The peanuts bring a lovely textural contrast to the bananas.

Serves 4

Ingredients:
600g green bananas – weight unpeeled
12 curry leaves
50g or 4tbsp. red skinned peanuts
2 tbsp. sesame seeds
2 whole green chillies – or to taste

For the tarka:
3 tbsp. oil
2 tsp cumin seeds

For the curry:
120g passata or chopped tomatoes
1 tsp jaggery – crumbled
1 tsp Himalayan salt
150ml boiling water

For the garnish:
2 tbsp. lemon juice
1 tbsp. roughly chopped roasted peanuts
Fresh coriander finely chopped

1. Peel and chop the green bananas into a bowl of salted water, and leave to soak for 10 minutes to allow their bitterness to release into water. Drain when ready to use.

2. Meanwhile, place the curry leaves, peanuts, sesame seeds, and chillies in the food processor bowl and blitz until they are finely powdered or just beginning to cream as the oil is released from the peanuts and the sesame. Set aside.

3. Heat the oil in a deep saucepan on a low to medium heat. Add the cumin seeds, and sizzle for a few seconds before adding the ground peanut mix. Stir into the oil and cook on a very low heat for 5 minutes, being careful not to burn the mixture and stirring it occasionally to distribute the heat through the mixture.

4. Add the drained bananas, tomatoes, jaggery and salt and stir through the peanut mixture. Cook on a low heat with the lid on until the bananas are cooked and the tomatoes have lost their acidity. Insert the end of a sharp knife into the bananas to check their tenderness; they should have the consistency of cooked potato.

5. Now add about 150ml boiling water or as you much as you need to get the sauce to your preferred consistency. Cook for a few minutes to incorporate all the flavours into the liquid.

6. Add the lemon juice, peanuts and fresh coriander, stir through and switch off the heat.

7. Serve with chapattis or with rice.

Salads & Chutneys

Salads, chutneys and pickles are an essential accompaniment to Indian meals; a good chutney could be happily eaten as a light snack or meal replacement with a freshly made paratha or poppadum, transforming a simple dish into something really vibrant, colourful and deliciously explosive. Since snacky foods, chaats or light bites are very much part of eating a meal, so too are the accompanying sauces, dips and chutneys.

The word chutney originates from the Hindi word 'chatni' for sauces usually made from local and seasonal fruits and spices with an old family recipe. As ever, this is a family or even a neighbourhood occasion, where locals will come together to share in the joy of a harvest.

The recipes are always ad lib and so will never be repeated twice in exactly the same way. Pickles are a great means of making good of a harvest of fruit to be consumed later in the year when such fruits are no longer available.

The abundant use of spices is designed to preserve the fruits and bring all of the flavours together as a tantalizing explosion, exploring every bit of your palate. Tamarind, dates, mangoes and figs are commonly used ingredients with lemon, sugar, chillies and oil. Contrary to popular belief, salads are also a requisite part of every meal.

Red onions, carrots, cucumbers and radishes mixed through with a pinch of salt, a squeeze of lime and a dusting of roasted ground cumin are as simple as it gets and assured to grace any table. Yoghurt is also a rudimentary part of a meal designed to provide a cooling agent and line the stomach to offset against any impending heat from the chillies.

Sliced Apple – for Salad Garnish

My father always ate an apple on a plate with a little pile of black pepper to the side which is where I discovered the joy of black pepper with apples. The lemon juice is used to prevent the apples from oxidization and one would imagine that it would bring sharpness to the dish, whereas the lemon simply cancels out the acidity in the apple, resulting in a wonderful balance of flavours.

Serves 4

Ingredients:
1 Braeburn, Cox's or Gala apple sliced into julienne strips
1 tbsp. of lemon juice
⅛ tsp coarsely ground black pepper

1. Place the apple in a small bowl.

2. Add the lemon juice and black pepper and mix well.

Serving Tips:

1. *Serve as a salad garnish or with chutney on the side.*

2. *Serve this apple salad with my chilli and fennel chicken dish or with the Goan salmon recipe. Mix with a few salad leaves; it adds a refreshing crunch.*

Tamarind & Date Chutney

This chutney is the genesis of brown sauce hailing from the days of the Raj, the era of British rule in India. The officers and expats loved the flavour of tamarind sauce so much that they re-created a recipe that was served in the restaurants of the Houses of Parliament. Brown sauce is part of the rich fabric of British culinary culture but its roots lie in the heart of India. My recipe uses dates to replace some of the traditional jaggery content to add further depth of flavour and nutritional value in the form of copper and magnesium.

Ingredients:

200g seedless tamarind

150g dates pitted and chopped finely

1½ litres of water (but to taste – depends on how thick or thin you want the sauce)

3 tsp roasted ground cumin

½ tsp salt or to taste

½ tsp hot chilli powder

3 tsp paprika or mild Kashmiri chilli powder (Kashmiri chilli powder has a very rich natural red colouring)

100g jaggery

1. Place the tamarind and dates into a deep pan with 1½ litres of boiling water. Bring to the boil, then drop the temperature and simmer gently for about an hour, stirring occasionally. Cook until the tamarind and dates have dissolved and are very tender.

2. Now add the cumin, salt, hot chilli powder, paprika or Kashmiri chilli powder and jaggery and stir well. Cook this out for a further 30 minutes on a low heat. Taste and adjust the seasoning to your taste; it will sweeten further as time goes on.

3. Pour into a very fine sieve and pass through to remove any coarse bits and remaining seeds. Use the back of a wooden spoon to mash into the sieve to refine it further and help it pass.

4. Allow to cool and preserve in a jar or squeezy bottle in the fridge. However the volume you have made will enable you to freeze some as well; pour into a Ziploc bag and thin out and freeze flat. This will enable you to take out chunks at a time as you need it.

Chef's Tips:

1. *Shelf life in the freezer is comfortably 18 months.*

2. *You may end up adding more water at the sieving process in order to strain out as much as possible; the main chutney still has enough integrity to carry it.*

Coriander & Mint Chutney

I love this chutney; it's zingy, it's fresh, it's tangy and as hot as you want it to be. Enjoy it with samosas, pakoras, bhajias or simply spread over a piping hot paratha. Heaven!

Serves 4

Ingredients:

15 mint leaves or to taste, but start with 15 – it may suit your mint tolerance

15 full stalks of coriander – complete with leaf and stalk

¼ medium white onion or 2 shallots – optional, peeled and chopped

½ or 1 green chilli – depending on your heat tolerance

1 tsp ginger, roughly chopped

1 tbsp. sesame seeds

2 tbsp. red skinned peanuts – smashed

2 tsp ground cumin

½ tsp salt or to taste

½ tsp sugar – optional to balance out the acidity

1 tbsp. lemon juice or 1 small fresh lemon

2 tbsp. natural yoghurt

1 tbsp. cold water (may not be needed)

1. Place all of the ingredients, minus the yoghurt, into the food processor bowl and blitz into a fine paste.

2. Add the yoghurt and blitz once more to incorporate the flavours consistently. You may need to add water if the consistency is a little thick; this will depend on the freshness of the leaves and consistency of the yoghurt when added.

3. Taste and adjust the seasoning of salt or chilli according to taste.

4. Add more water or yoghurt to take the chutney to the right consistency.

5. Serve and enjoy!

Chef's Tips:

1. *If you have a peanut allergy, simply miss them out.*

2. *This chutney may be stored in the deep freeze in a Ziploc bag.*

3. *Be sure to use a probiotic yoghurt with live cultures to build up your good bacteria.*

Coconut Chutney

This is a traditional south Indian chutney that accompanies dosa, idli and street foods. I would always recommend using fresh coconut where possible, though the frozen 'fresh coconut' can be an emergency substitute where necessary. The curry leaves are double layered in this dish, appearing in the main body as well as in the tarka infusion, and this brings an added fragrance that essentially makes this dish.

Ingredients:
½ fresh coconut, shelled and skin removed
1 fresh green finger chilli
15 curry leaves
7 strands fresh coriander
¼ tsp salt
¼ tsp ground cumin
2 tbsp. of lemon juice
2-3 tbsp. of thick Greek yoghurt or to taste to loosen the chutney

For the tarka:
1 tbsp. vegetable oil
1 tsp black mustard seeds
1 tsp white urid lentils
2 red dried whole chillies
10 curry leaves

1. Place the coconut, green chilli, curry leaves, fresh coriander, salt, cumin and lemon juice into a blender and blitz into a fine but thick paste.

2. Now add the yoghurt and blend once more. Add more yoghurt if required to achieve the required consistency.

3. To make the tarka, heat the oil and add the mustard seeds; allow the seeds to pop then add the lentils then the whole dried chillies and curry leaves. Sizzle for at least 1 minute on a low heat.

4. Pour into the coconut chutney and mix.

5. Check the salt and lemon juice to taste.

Fresh Turmeric & Mustard Relish

This is the Indian equivalent of piccalilli with its roots firmly in the heart of north west India. Its strong flavour tones lend it to being eaten quite simply with Indian breads and kachumber or it is equally delicious as an accompaniment to a traditional English ploughman's. Nutritionally speaking this is a powerhouse of medicinal properties designed to keep the germs at bay!

Ingredients:

100g fresh white turmeric

50g fresh yellow turmeric (use 150g of yellow if that's all you can find)

50g fresh ginger

10g green chillies – hot variety (or 3-4 3 inches long) though reduce this to start with on your first batch and see how you go...

4 tsp yellow mustard seeds (mustard will also provide heat)

4 tbsp. lemon juice (I use bottled lemon juice)

½ tsp salt or to taste

5 tsp caster sugar (not jaggery as it changes the colour and texture of the chutney)

4 tbsp. oil (not extra-virgin olive oil)

1. Scrape the turmeric and ginger and give it a quick wipe to take off any rough bits.

2. Place all of the ingredients into a food processor and blend until you have a fine paste – a similar consistency to a tapenade or pesto sauce.

3. Place in a clean/sterilized jar and store in the refrigerator.

Serving Tips:

1. *Serve with a good piece of ham or cheese.*

2. *Add a teaspoon to a vegetable soup to give it a little lift and extra flavour.*

3. *Use as a sandwich filling – sparingly – it can be quite hot!*

Apple Chundo

This is a popular lip smacking accompaniment to theplas (a traditional Gujarati fenugreek flat bread made from a combination of whole wheat flour and chickpea flour mixed with spices and fenugreek leaves).

Traditionally apple or mango chundo, also known as chatni in Hindi, was made by keeping the combination of grated raw mangoes or apples and jaggery in a large covered glass jar in the sun for several days. The heat of the sun would dissolve the sugar and slowly the grated fruit acquired a delicious translucent colour. The recipe below is for the chundo prepared using jaggery instead of sugar.

Ingredients:
500g grated raw apples
1 inch piece of raw fresh ginger
1 tsp sea salt
1 tsp turmeric powder
200g jaggery – crumbled or grated
1½ tsp ground roasted cumin powder
1 tsp chilli powder

1. Mix the grated apples, ginger, salt and turmeric powder in a bowl and set aside for 15 minutes so that the salt and turmeric permeates into the apples.

2. Now add the grated jaggery little by little, combining all the ingredients together.

3. Then heat a pan and slowly sauté the mixture until all the jaggery is completely dissolved and the chundo thickens.

4. Add the cumin at this point and stir in well.

5. When the bubbles appear and the grated apple begins to glisten with the jaggery syrup and thickens, remove from the heat.

6. Allow the mixture to cool before spooning into clean sterilized jars.

Chef's Tips:

1. This fresh dip will keep for up to 4 days refrigerated.

2. Makes a great healthy option salad dressing.

3. You could use crème fraîche instead of yoghurt.

Cucumber, Coconut & Curry Leaf Salad

The tarka is an essential part of this dish as it serves to really accentuate the freshness of the ingredients. This salad is best served straight away once the tarka is added as the ingredients can deteriorate quickly. If you wish to enjoy it without the tarka just stir the curry leaves through – it will still be delicious.

Serves 4 as s side dish

Ingredients:
½ cucumber, centre seeds scooped out, and cut into julienne
2 tbsp. grated coconut
2 tbsp. coriander leaves, chopped
1 green chilli – finely sliced into julienne
Zest and juice of a lime
Salt to taste

1 tbsp. oil
1 tsp mustard seeds
8 curry leaves

1. Cut the cucumber into 2 inch pieces then cut in half lengthways, scoop out the seeds and cut into thin julienne strips, about the size of bean sprout shoots, and place in a bowl.

2. Now add the grated coconut, fresh coriander, finely sliced green chilli, lime zest and juice of the lime and a pinch of salt to taste. Toss together and set aside.

3. In a tarka pan or high-sided sauté pan gently heat the oil for a few seconds before adding the mustard seeds. Ensure the mustard seeds have finished popping and then add the curry leaves. Allow the tarka to infuse the seeds and then pour over the salad. Toss to mix through and serve.

Chef's Tip:

Use courgettes if you prefer.

Carrot & Mustard Salad

Whilst carrots already have a sweet and pleasant flavour and are often enjoyed as crudités, I think the dip is all too often the incentive to eat them. So here's a perfect example of how a simple tarka (infusion) can elevate the flavours to another level, making the dish really quite moreish. The hot spicy oil infused with mustard seeds is tempered by the lemon juice, chillies and a degree of sweetness from the sugar. I often add the long thin radishes to this recipe when in season.

Serves 4 as s side dish

Ingredients:
4 small carrots – scrubbed and cut into 1½ inch thin batons
3 x 2 inch pieces fresh turmeric, peeled and washed
5 long green chillies – washed and dried
2 tbsp. rapeseed oil
2 tsp mustard seeds
½ tsp asafoetida
10 curry leaves
½ tsp mango powder
1 tsp sugar
2 tbsp. lemon juice

1. Scrub the carrots, drain and towel dry. Cut into thin batons 1½ inches long. Set aside.

2. Peel and prepare the fresh turmeric, slice in half lengthways (I would recommend wearing gloves as it may stain your fingers during the preparation). Add to the bowl with the carrots.

3. Wash and dry the green chillies and slice downwards lengthways almost to the top of the chilli but not quite to keep the chilli whole. Set aside.

4. In a sauté pan heat the oil, and when it's hot add the mustard seeds and sizzle until they finish popping. Turn down the temperature very low, then add the asafoetida, followed by the curry leaves, mango powder, sugar and lemon juice. Stir well and toss in the chillies. Sauté for 30 seconds then remove from the heat. Allow to cool.

5. When cooled add the carrots and fresh turmeric and toss the ingredients to allow the spices to mix into the vegetables. Stored in a sterile glass jar this will keep in the fridge for up to two weeks.

Kachumber

Kachumber is perhaps one of the most common salads particularly in the northern states of India, Maharashtra and Gujarat. It is a dish that can turn the humble and sometimes overlooked cucumber into a vivid and vibrant zingy salad. Add to that the guest appearance of a number of other seemingly unassuming characters like lime, cumin and red onion and as a whole they combine to create something utterly delicious. I think it's the equivalent of a simple Greek salad, eaten and served in much the same way.

Serves 4 as s side dish

Ingredients:
1 cucumber, deseeded and diced
½ small red onion, finely diced
4 baby radishes, cubed
10 baby plum tomatoes, deseeded and cut into small cubes
6 springs of mint – leaves only – chopped
2 tbsp. fresh coriander, finely chopped
1 lime, juiced
¼ tsp chilli flakes

2 tsp cumin seeds, roasted and coarsely ground
Pinch of Himalayan salt to taste

1. Prepare all the vegetables, fresh herbs and lime juice as described in the ingredients list and place them into a bowl. Add the chilli flakes and mix well.

2. Toast the cumin seeds in a dry frying pan for about a minute; you should be able to really smell their aroma, but go easy, as they can burn very quickly.

3. Very lightly smash the cumin seeds in a mortar and pestle or with a rolling pin.

4. Scatter the cumin seeds over the salad. Add a pinch of salt.

5. Serve and enjoy the fresh zingy flavours.

Raita – Fresh Yoghurt & Cucumber Dressing

This is the most quintessential yoghurt dressing that can be found throughout most of India: cool and refreshing, it is served alongside most meals. The recipe will vary slightly from home to home and should be adjusted to your own preference. I would suggest using the thickest yoghurt available and most definitely a probiotic to bolster up the immune system.

Serves 4

Ingredients:

8 heaped tsp plain Greek yoghurt or natural bio yoghurt

4 tsp cucumber, grated (if it's very sloppy squeeze some of the water out)

½ tsp freshly ground black pepper

Salt to season and taste

Large pinch of freshly chopped coriander

½ tsp of roasted cumin (optional)

1. Mix all of the ingredients together. Turn the raita into a serving bowl.

2. Enjoy!

Chef's Tips:

1. This fresh dip will keep for up to 4 days refrigerated.

2. Makes a great healthy option salad dressing.

3. You could use crème fraîche instead of yoghurt.

Sweet Capsicum & Chilli Salsa

A flavour explosion on the palate is the only way to describe this salsa. I could genuinely eat this just as it is or perhaps with some leftover chapattis made into flatbreads. It's almost like the Indian version of the Spanish tortilla with a salsa dip.

Ingredients:
1 large red capsicum, deseeded and cored
1 medium carrot, peeled
3 tomatoes, deseeded
½ cucumber, deseeded
1 hot red chilli or green chilli, very finely chopped
2 limes, juiced
2 tbsp. jaggery
¼ tsp Himalayan salt or to taste
2 tsp toasted cumin seeds, roughly ground
2 tbsp. fresh coriander, finely chopped

1. Wash and finely dice the capsicum and carrot into 3mm cubes.

2. Deseed the tomatoes and cucumber and finely dice into 3mm cubes. Chop the chilli very finely.

3. Mix the capsicum, carrot, tomatoes, cucumber and chilli in a bowl.

4. Grind the lime juice, jaggery, salt and toasted cumin seeds in a pestle and mortar until smooth.

5. Mix the dressing into the salsa and add the fresh coriander.

6. If the salsa is too runny strain some of the juices off – you should be able to spoon it onto a bhel biscuit or add it to a leaf salad.

7. Turn out into a serving bowl.

8. Serve.

Lentils & Pulses

Pulses form the basis of day-to-day Indian cooking. They are an essential part of an Indian diet and revered for their health-giving properties such as iron, fibre and protein, which are important to a vegetarian diet.

Daal, as it is often referred to, encompasses the broad term for beans, pulses and peas. Though beans for some reason are usually referred to by their specific name, such as kidney beans (rajma), whereas when the daal is split and shelled, it is often referred to in a more generic term as a daal (stripped of its authority name).

Daals are cooked to a broth or casserole-like consistency depending on the size of bean and usually eaten with chapattis, rotis, paratha, or rice. In addition, when you eat it with the bread component it becomes a complete protein and also a wonderful satisfying meal.

It is often considered as a side dish, but I don't think so. With a great tarka, the flavours can stand their ground any day and a good piece of bread to scoop it up with is a joyous eating experience.

The Western diet can be dismissive of lentils as they are often viewed as a boring ingredient. However the judicious use of spices can transform them into something truly magnificent, both in terms of taste and nutritional value.

Furthermore they are very cost-effective proteins that have few environmental implications in their production, making them an excellent alternative to meats.

Don't be put off from using canned lentils; they retain a high proportion of their goodness, with only 1g or percent nutrient diminishment than the dried version, which is negligible in reality, and because they are precooked you can create a meal in no time at all.

Moong Daal

The moong bean, otherwise known as the split yellow daal, is native to India. It is the most common of the lentil family and is eaten in a very simple way with chapattis or as a side dish. It has a wonderful buttery taste and is my go-to for soothing comfort food at any time of the year. They say soup is food for the soul but I'd say a simple mung daal broth comes pretty close.

In this recipe I've cooked it almost like a flavoured rice dish using the absorption method. It would be perfect to accompany a fish dish.

Serves 4

Ingredients:
200g moong daal
½ tsp turmeric
½ tsp salt
¼ tsp asafoetida
5 curry leaves
½ tsp fresh green chilli, finely chopped
1 tsp finely chopped ginger
2 tsp of oil or ghee
3 strands of spring onions, finely chopped (white and green parts separated)
3 strands of fresh coriander

1. Sort through the moong daal to ensure that there are no stones amongst the daal.

2. Wash the daal in warm water, changing the water several times to ensure all the chalky residue has washed away. Now soak the daal for 1 hour if time permits.

3. Place the washed daal into a saucepan with 300ml of hot water, add the turmeric, salt, asafoetida, curry leaves, green chilli, ginger, ghee and the white part of the spring onions, reserving the green part for garnishing later. Mix well and bring to the boil or boiling point on a medium heat.

4. Now turn the heat down to a low simmering point, place the lid on the pan and cook for 20 minutes or until all of the water has been absorbed. The daal should be soft and broken down to an almost slightly mushy consistency.

5. Add the remaining green part of the spring onions and a little fresh coriander to garnish; serve with hot chapattis to accompany a main course fish meal.

Channa Masala

Channa or chole originates from the northern region of India. You may know it as channa masala in your local restaurant. It is a dry dish with a sour citrus note and is usually favoured by vegetarians as a go-to staple. In the Punjab region in north India channa masala is often served with 'bhutura' – a fluffy fried bread made from wheat flour and yoghurt, and it's a beautiful pairing.

I am perfectly happy to use the canned variety and I would not be inclined to rinse the lentils as the juices they have been sat in contain all the goodness of the bean. In my version I have omitted the onions to speed up the recipe; instead I've added gram flour to thicken the dish. The dried fenugreek leaves will add immense depth and flavour.

Serves 6

Ingredients:
3 tbsp. oil
1 large cinnamon stick
1 tsp whole cumin seeds
½ tsp asafoetida
2 tbsp. gram flour
2 tsp finely chopped garlic
3 tsp finely chopped ginger
200g tinned chopped tomatoes or passata
1 tsp tomato puree
2 tsp ground cumin
1 tsp ground coriander
½ tsp turmeric
½ tsp hot chilli powder or taste
1 tsp jaggery
1 tsp Himalayan salt or to taste
¼ tsp garam masala
2 tbsp. fresh coriander
1 tbsp. dried fenugreek leaves
400g boiled chickpeas or 2 tins of canned chickpeas
100-150ml hot water or to preferred consistency
1 tbsp. lemon juice

1. Heat the oil in a pan, and when hot add the cinnamon stick and cumin seeds, sizzling for a few seconds before adding the asafoetida quickly followed by the gram flour. Turn the heat off and cook the gram flour for about a minute, stirring well to ensure that it doesn't stick or burn. The latent heat will be sufficient (gram flour burns very quickly).

2. Turn the heat on to low and add the garlic and ginger; infuse with the cinnamon and cumin for about 2 minutes before adding the tomatoes and puree and then increase the temperature to medium to bring the sauce to a simmer. Return to a lower heat once it has regained simmering temperature.

3. When the oil begins to separate and the water has evaporated from the tomatoes, lower the heat and add the spices: ground cumin, coriander, turmeric, chilli powder, jaggery, salt, garam masala, half of the fresh coriander and the dried fenugreek. Cook the spices over a gentle heat for 5 minutes.

4. Add the chickpeas and stir through ensuring the chickpeas are thoroughly coated. Keep the temperature on a gentle heat, and cook for 5 minutes with the lid on to allow the spices to meld into the chickpeas and cook with the steam as well as the heat. Add a little water to create a sauce if necessary, dependent on the consistency you may prefer.

5. Garnish with lemon juice and the remaining fresh coriander or strips of ginger if you prefer. Serve with chapatti or puris.

Black-Eyed Peas with Aubergine

Nothing to do with the American pop band that was, but these lentils are very much enjoyed by a number of the Southern American states. Although they are referred to as black-eyed peas, they are in fact a bean. Whilst being higher in carbohydrates than many other lentils they have higher iron content and are great for fighting inflammatory conditions and lowering blood pressure. Black-eyed peas have a nutty, earthy and creamy flavour, whilst being buttery in texture. In my recipe I've added aubergine as it helps to reduce the gassy effect of lentils and gives provides further depth of flavour. The beans are best soaked overnight or for at least 6 hours to speed up the cooking process.

Serves 4

Ingredients:
200g black-eyed beans
1 large aubergine – diced into 1 inch cubes
½ tsp turmeric

Wet herb paste:
3 medium tomatoes
2 medium onions, finely chopped
2 tsp fresh garlic, finely chopped
2 tsp ginger, finely chopped
2 tbsp. fresh coconut, grated

For the tarka:
2 tbsp. oil
1 tsp cumin seeds
¼ tsp asafoetida

Powdered spices:
½ tsp chilli powder
2 tsp ground coriander
1 tsp ground cumin
½ tsp turmeric
½ tsp garam masala
1 tsp salt
150ml boiling water

Fresh lemon juice to finish
5-6 stalks of fresh coriander, finely chopped to garnish

1. Soak the beans in warm water overnight.

2. When ready to use, rinse thoroughly and transfer to a pressure cooker along with the cubed aubergine and turmeric. Cook for 6-8 whistles or boil in a deep heavy-based pan for 45 minutes with just enough water to cover the beans.

3. Meanwhile, place the tomato, onion, garlic, ginger and coconut into a food processor or mortar and pestle and grind to a smooth paste and set aside.

4. Now for the tarka, heat the oil in a deep pan, add the cumin seeds and sizzle for a few seconds before adding the asafoetida followed by the paste. Stir well in the oil and cook for 3-4 minutes before adding the chilli powder, ground coriander, ground cumin, turmeric, garam masala and salt. Stir continuously for a minute to mix the flavours into one another.

5. Add the cooked black-eyed beans, stir once more and cook for 5 minutes then add 150ml boiling water and simmer with the lid on for 15 minutes on a low heat.

6. Finish with a little fresh lemon juice, garnish with fresh coriander leaves and serve hot with chapattis or parathas.

Tarka Daal

This dish is so synonymous with an Indian restaurant menu, and a very popular dish with our customers here at The Cooking Academy. I've no idea why the restaurants call this dish tarka daal, given that tarka refers to a cooking process rather than to a particular recipe. Unlike many of the other lentil recipes in this book i.e. moong daal, any type of yellow lentil can be used in this recipe and the tarka element is merely the process of creating an infusion using oil and seeds or whole spices which will then infuse and impart the flavour into the oil and the rest of the dish very quickly. And since the dish has so few other ingredients it is heavily reliant upon the tarka for flavour.

Serves 4

Ingredients:
200g yellow moong daal
100g split channa daal
1 litre of hot water
½ tsp turmeric
1½ tsp salt or to taste
2 tsp fresh ginger, finely chopped
2 fresh green chillies, minced
Handful of fresh coriander, finely chopped

For the tarka:
2 tbsp. oil
1 tsp black mustard seeds
1 tsp cumin seeds
½ tsp asafoetida
1 tsp minced garlic
1 or 2 whole green chillies slit to ¾ of the way up

1. Wash and soak the daal for 1 hour in boiling water, then drain and transfer it into a large pan with a litre of hot water and add the turmeric and the salt. Bring to the boil over a high heat, spooning off any frothy scum on the surface. Reduce the heat to low and simmer for 20 minutes, or until all the daal is soft. You may need to top up the water depending on the rate of moisture evaporation.

2. Once cooked add the finely chopped ginger and minced green chillies, and mix well so that they are incorporated into the daal.

3. Add a tablespoon of fresh coriander, finely chopped. Set aside.

4. For the tarka: Heat the oil in a separate saucepan, and when the oil is hot add the mustard seeds. Wait for them to finish popping before adding the cumin seeds; lower the temperature then add the asafoetida and the minced garlic. Remove from the heat to avoid the garlic overcooking, and stir the whole green chillies into the oil and sizzle for a few seconds before pouring the daal into the tarka. Stir well and put back on the heat to cook for a few minutes for the flavours to soak in, then decant into a serving bowl.

Chef's Tip:

You could use just the moong daal if you would prefer a smoother texture.

Panchmel Daal of Rajasthan

The somewhat inhospitable desert of Rajasthan has challenged man's culinary creativity. Water was a scare resource, and so their ability to grow their own crops was very limited. Ingredients such as rice and green vegetables were an imported luxury. And so this region has heavily relied upon dried foods such as lentils, game meat that can survive such dry terrain, and pickles to liven up the dinner plate. Panch is the Hindi word for five, and so this recipe is about using five different types of lentils to give different levels of texture and flavour in a single mouthful.

Serves 4

Ingredients:
60g tuwar daal
60g urid daal
60g chana daal
60g masoor daal
60g whole mung daal
500ml boiling water
1 tsp turmeric
½ tsp salt or to taste

For the tarka:
1 tbsp. oil
3 cloves
2 tsp cumin seeds
2-3 whole dried chillies or to taste
¼ tsp asafoetida
2 tsp finely chopped garlic
2 tsp finely chopped ginger
2 tsp ground cumin
2 tsp ground coriander
1 tsp Kashmiri chilli powder
1 tsp paprika
2 medium tomatoes, deseeded and chopped finely
2 tbsp. fresh coriander, finely chopped

1. Wash the daal in hand-hot water and leave to soak in double the quantity of water to daal for at least 2 hours, or overnight if possible.

2. When you are ready to cook, drain the daal and then add 500ml of boiling water to a large saucepan with the daal, along with the turmeric and the salt. Bring to the boil and then simmer on a low temperature with the lid on until they are tender; check a little of the daal to be sure. You will need to check the water level from time to time to ensure that they do not dry up. Alternatively cook in a pressure cooker to speed up the process.

3. Heat the oil in a saucepan. Add the cloves, cumin seeds, dried chillies and asafoetida. Immediately add the garlic and ginger and cook for one minute on a low heat. Then add the ground cumin and coriander, chilli powder and paprika, stirring gently as you go to mix all the spices together. Cook for another minute on a low heat.

4. Add the tomatoes and stir to incorporate all the flavours. Cook until the tomatoes have softened and most of water from the tomatoes has evaporated.

5. Add the daal, stir well and bring to the boil, adding water as preferred if the daal is too thick. Adjust the seasoning of salt and chilli to taste. Simmer for 10 minutes over a low heat. Remove from the heat and garnish with fresh coriander.

6. Serve with hot chapattis or parathas.

Daal Makhani

Daal makhani is truly the king of daal. The word makhan means cream and the cream comes from not only the addition at the end of the cooking process but also the way the lentils are cooked over a long period of time to tease out their buttery and nutty essence. Traditionally this dish was cooked overnight by the chefs in royal households. This is a truly luxurious way of cooking and eating lentils and worthy of the effort involved.

Serves 4

Ingredients:

170g dried whole urid lentils
40g dried kidney beans
1 tbsp. oil
30g butter
3 cloves
1 small cinnamon stick
2 green cardamoms
1 black cardamom
1 bay leaf
1 large onion finely chopped
1 tsp minced garlic
1 tsp minced ginger
½ tsp chopped green chilli
½ tsp ground cumin
½ tsp ground coriander
¼ tsp hot chilli powder
¼ tsp garam masala
¼ tsp ground nutmeg
1 tsp salt
1 tbsp. dried fenugreek leaves
1 x 3-finger pinch chopped fresh coriander
150ml pureed tomatoes (tinned are ok – but blitz in a processor first)
50ml water (optional)
2 tbsp. single cream

1. Soak the urid lentils and kidney beans overnight in double the quantity of water to lentils/beans. Drain the water and cook them together in fresh water (about 3 times the quantity of lentils) without salt on a low heat with the lid on the saucepan for 2-3 hours. Keep stirring every 15 minutes so it doesn't catch at the bottom. Top up with fresh boiling water during the cooking process if needed. Once both are cooked to soft but not mushy consistency, turn off the heat and set aside.

2. In another saucepan add the oil and butter and heat on a low heat. When the butter is melted and sizzling, add the whole spices and cook for a minute (cloves, cinnamon stick, green cardamoms, black cardamom and bay leaf).

3. Now add the onion and gently sweat it until it is translucent, for about 8-10 minutes. Add the garlic, ginger and green chilli and cook for a further 2 minutes to infuse the flavours.

4. Now add the ground cumin, ground coriander, hot chilli powder, garam masala, nutmeg, salt, dried fenugreek leaves and a large finger pinch of freshly chopped coriander.

5. Mix well and continue to cook on a low flame, roasting all the spices and allowing them to infuse into the onion mixture. Add the pureed tomatoes and mix to incorporate them into the spice mixture.

6. Now add the cooked lentils and kidney beans and mix well. Continue to cook everything on a low heat for another 15 minutes with a lid on. If the mixture is too thick, add 50ml water as the daal is meant to be of medium consistency.

7. When all the ingredients have come together, finish off with the cream and switch off the heat. Serve hot.

Serving Tip:

Garnish with a swirl of cream and some fine julienne of ginger on top over some hot basmati rice, or serve with any Indian flatbreads.

Spinach Daal (Palak Daal)

Palak is the Hindi name for spinach and when paired with lentils it creates a protein packed dish and a complete meal in itself. The mildly bitter flavour of the spinach is complemented by the buttery notes of the channa daal. Although I am using the split gram in this recipe, chickpeas work equally well here. The use of ghee brings an extra luxurious feel to this dish and is absorbed really well because of the spinach.

Serves 4

Ingredients:
150g channa daal (split gram)
500g fresh spinach
2 tbsp. ghee or oil
1 medium onion, finely chopped
2 tsp fresh ginger, finely chopped
1 tsp finely chopped green finger chillies
2 tomatoes, finely chopped, loose seeds removed
1 tsp ground coriander
¼ tsp hot chilli powder
½ tsp salt
300ml hot water

5-6 stalks of fresh coriander, finely chopped
Pinch of garam masala to garnish

1. Soak the daal in warm water for 2-3 hours.

2. When ready to use, rinse thoroughly and strain through a fine sieve.

3. Wash the spinach thoroughly, remove the stems and discard, finely chop the spinach and set aside.

4. In a deep heavy-based pan, add the ghee or oil and fry the onion on a low heat until it is lightly golden.

5. Now add the strained lentils, the spinach, ginger, chillies, tomatoes and ground coriander, hot chilli powder and salt as well as the water.

6. Bring to the boil and simmer gently for 30 minutes or pressure cook for 2-3 whistles.

7. When the daal is cooked, lightly mash the lentils using a fork.

8. Add the fresh coriander and pinch of garam masala to garnish.

9. Enjoy with fresh chapattis.

Rajma Lentils – Punjabi Kidney Bean Curry

Although kidney beans are commonly associated with the South American subcontinent, it may come as a surprise to realise that they are also quite popular in Indian cuisine. They have a meaty and satisfying texture and when you remove the skin the bean has a delightfully smooth and almost creamy flesh which is what makes them comfort food.

Hearty and tasty is the only way to describe this bowl of loveliness; the tarka really brings the dish into its own. You could finish with a dollop of cream if you're feeling a little indulgent.

Serves 4

Ingredients:
250g dried red kidney beans or
2 cans of cooked kidney beans,
drained and rinsed
1 green finger chilli, finely chopped
1 inch piece of ginger, finely sliced
½ tsp bicarbonate of soda

For the tarka:
2 tbsp. oil
1 tsp cumin seeds
8 curry leaves
¼ tsp asafoetida
1 medium onion, finely chopped
2 tsp fresh garlic, finely chopped
1 tsp ginger, finely chopped
1 tsp ground coriander
1 tsp ground cumin
½ tsp turmeric
¼ tsp garam masala
½ tsp Kashmiri chilli powder
1 tsp salt
100g fresh fenugreek, finely chopped
5-6 stalks of fresh coriander, finely chopped
2 large tomatoes, finely chopped
100ml water

For the garnish:
Handful fresh coriander to garnish
Fresh ginger, sliced into matchsticks
Pinch of garam masala to garnish

1. Soak the dried kidney beans in hot water overnight. Alternatively you can use 2 cans of cooked kidney beans.

2. When ready to use, rinse thoroughly and transfer to a pressure cooker along with the green chilli, sliced ginger and bicarbonate of soda. Cook for 6-8 whistles or alternatively boil in a deep heavy-based pan for 45 minutes in 1 litre of water. Be careful not to overboil. Strain through a fine sieve.

3. For the tarka, heat 2 tablespoons of oil in a pan, add the cumin seeds followed by the curry leaves and asafoetida and then the onion. Cook for 5-7 minutes until golden brown, before adding the rest of the spices: garlic, ginger, ground coriander, ground cumin, turmeric, garam masala, Kashmiri chilli powder and salt along with the finely chopped fresh fenugreek and fresh coriander.

4. Gently cook for 5 minutes on a low heat being careful not to burn the spices, then stir in the chopped tomatoes. Raise the temperature until the tomatoes start to sizzle, then turn it down again and continue to cook on a gentle heat for 5-7 minutes until the oil begins to separate.

5. Now add the kidney beans; stir and cook for a few minutes on a low heat before adding 100ml of water. Stir in and cook on a low heat for 10-15 minutes until the spices have soaked into the beans and the sauce has become consistent.

6. Garnish with fresh coriander, ginger matchsticks and a pinch of garam masala.

7. Enjoy with fresh chapattis or naan bread.

Mixed Beans & Pulses Medley

My first dalliance with this recipe was at the dinner table of my dear friend and partner in food indulgence, Hash Patel. She hadn't intended to serve this with our meal, thinking it too simple to please my palate, but instead I enjoyed every spoonful of the hot, sweet and tangy delicious flavours. I've made the dish many times over in my own home and introduced it into our vegetarian cookery class.

I adore the convenience of canned lentils and their different flavours and textures as well as the speed with which a meal can be prepared. I also enjoy the randomness of being able to add any type of bean depending on what I find in the larder.

Serves 4 as a side dish

Ingredients:
100g canned sweetcorn
100g canned black-eyed peas
100g canned chickpeas
100g canned kidney beans
100g pinto beans (or any other beans suitable for casseroles)
4 tbsp. vegetable oil
1 tsp bishop's weed seeds (ajwain)
½ tsp asafoetida
2 tbsp. gram flour
2 tbsp. ginger – finely chopped or julienne
1 tsp Kashmiri red chilli powder
2 tsp ground roasted cumin
2 tsp ground coriander
1 tsp jaggery
1 tsp Himalayan salt
1 heaped tsp tomato puree
2 tbsp. tamarind puree
1 tbsp. fresh coriander + 1 tbsp. to garnish
250-300ml hot/warm water
1 tbsp. fresh coriander

1. Open the cans, strain and set aside.

2. In a medium saucepan heat the oil and sauté the bishop's weed seeds for a few seconds (make sure the heat is very low or off once you have initially heated the oil) before adding the asafoetida and gram flour. Continue to cook the flour for a few minutes on a very low heat.

3. Now add the ginger, Kashmiri red chilli powder, ground cumin and coriander, jaggery, salt, tomato puree, tamarind puree and fresh coriander. Cook for about 5 minutes on a low heat – this will resemble a roux.

4. Add the sweetcorn/beans to the spice mix and stir gently to incorporate all of the flavours.

5. When it's all integrated add 250-300ml of boiling water and stir through. Allow the sauce to thicken and the water to be slightly absorbed into the beans.

6. Now add the remaining fresh coriander and serve with chapattis or naan bread.

Chef's Tip:

Use different beans/lentils to the ones above, based on your taste or availability.

Rice

In Hinduism, rice holds great spiritual and ritual significance as it is the staple grain of the Indian diet. Therefore it is no surprise that it is one of the world's largest producers of rice, cultivating nearly 20% of the world production. Rice is thought to have originated over 9,000 years ago at the foot of the Himalayas. Although there are many different types of rice the most well-known grain used in Indian cuisine is basmati, a long and slender grain giving a sweet and nutty flavour with a delicate and distinctive fragrance.

It is a common misconception that rice is traditionally served alongside main meal dishes. In Indian households rice would be served after the main event, possibly accompanied by a runny daal such as sambal or a sauce of some kind which may be the gravy element from the main course. The exception to this rule would be in the case of a kedgeree or biriyani which is the main focal point of the meal or even centrepiece.

Although rice tends to be thought of as an accompaniment in the West, in India it is eaten at all times of the day, for breakfast, lunch and dinner. For example for breakfast, rice is ground with lentils to make batter for dosas and idli. For street food, ground rice will form the batter for bhajia.

Furthermore there are also a large number of recipes where rice is an important ingredient in its own right. Probably most famous in the West is biriyani where rice is cooked together with meat or fish or vegetables.

Another such similar dish is khichdi, a dish with much history. Khichdi is a dish of rice and lentils revered as great comfort food. It is prepared all across northern India, Pakistan and further south where they add prawns or fish to the recipe. Perhaps the best known variation is kedgeree – rice, smoked fish, eggs and butter, the ultimate Anglo-Indian dish.

My rice recipes here are tried and trusted favourites, from a simple fragrant cumin infusion to the multi-layered biriyanis and pilafs. I hope you enjoy all the flavours.

Vegetable Pilaf Rice

As the title implies, the trick is to use any vegetables you wish; perhaps the most common would be the ones I have used below however I usually raid the fridge and use whatever I can lay my hands on. The stir-frying of the onions and spices is the most important step as you will develop flavour by taking your time over this process.

Serves 4

Ingredients:
200g basmati rice
½ medium carrot, peeled and finely diced
½ red capsicum, finely diced
2 tbsp. ghee
1 stick of cinnamon
1 medium onion, thinly sliced
½ tsp garlic, finely chopped
½ tsp ground roasted cumin
½ tsp ground coriander
¼ tsp turmeric
1 tsp salt
380ml hot water

To finish:
40g cooked peas

1. Wash the rice in warm to hand-hot water in a bowl until the water is clear. To do this start by swirling the grains of rice between your fingers in the water; by doing so you will loosen the cloudy starch from the grain and release it into the water. Drain off the water and repeat the process until the water eventually runs clear. This may take several changes of water, but it is worth it, as you reduce the starch content and therefore the calorific value of the rice. Set aside.

2. Finely dice the carrot and red capsicum. Set aside.

3. Melt the ghee in a medium saucepan. When the ghee is melted add the cinnamon stick followed by the onion, and cook for 5 minutes on a low heat until golden brown. Add the carrot and cook for 5 minutes on a low heat with the lid on.

4. Add the garlic and the cumin, coriander, turmeric and salt. Stir well to ensure all the flavours infuse into each other. Cook for 2-3 minutes on a low heat to ensure that the spices release their flavours but don't burn.

5. Now add the rice; stir in until all the rice is thoroughly coated in the spices and cook for 1 minute, before adding the hot water. Add the diced capsicum.

6. Bring up to the boil and simmer for a minute and then drop the temperature to the lowest point and simmer with the lid on for 10 minutes. Turn off the heat.

7. Remove from the heat and stir in the peas quickly to reduce the level of heat escaping from the pan. Replace the lid and rest for 10 minutes at least.

8. Serve immediately.

Chef's Tip:
Get extra health benefits by swapping to brown or wild rice.

Golden Saffron Rice

Saffron is a very delicate, aromatic, yet powerful spice and can very easily overpower a dish so be cautious with its use; even a few strands will add the flavour, whilst the crimson threads will contrast beautifully in the fullness of time. Don't be tempted to buy the cheaper brands; it comes through in the taste and seeing as you would use it so sparingly, it's worth investing in the good stuff.

Serves 4

Ingredients:
200g basmati rice
2 tbsp. ghee (clarified butter)
1 stick of cinnamon
1 star anise
3 green cardamom pods
8 curry leaves
1 medium onion – thinly sliced
½ tsp saffron
1 tsp salt
380ml hot water

To finish:
2 tbsp. fresh coriander – finely chopped

1. Wash the rice in warm to hand-hot water in a bowl until the water is clear. To do this start by swirling the grains of rice between your fingers in the water; by doing so you will loosen the cloudy starch from the grain and release it into the water. Drain off the water and repeat the process until the water eventually runs clear. This may take several changes of water, but it is worth it, as you reduce the starch content and therefore the calorific value of the rice. Drain in a sieve when ready to use.

2. Melt the ghee in a medium saucepan then add the cinnamon stick, star anise and cardamom pods and sizzle for a few seconds before adding the curry leaves immediately followed by the onion. Stir to soak the onion in the infused oil and cook for 5 minutes on a low heat until caramelizing and golden brown.

3. Now add the saffron, stir and cook for a minute before adding the salt and rice and stir-fry for 2-3 minutes on a medium heat to ensure all the flavours infuse into each other, until all the liquid has evaporated and you are effectively dry-frying the rice.

4. Now add the hot water, bring up to the boil and simmer for a minute and then drop the temperature to the lowest point and simmer with the lid on for 10 minutes. Turn off the heat and stand for another 10 minutes.

5. When you are ready to serve, decant into a serving dish and stir in the fresh coriander.

6. Serve immediately.

Chef's Tips:

1. *Adding the saffron just a minute ahead of the rice is hugely beneficial in developing the flavours.*

2. *Garnish with pre-fried onions for extra texture.*

Khichiri (otherwise known as Kedgeree)

Some call it kedgeree; for others it is of course khichiri, a dish whose origins are steeped in history, traced back to at least the 1300s. Men who worked for the British East India Company wrote about how delicious khichiri was as early as the late 17th century, perhaps a throwback to the comfort of nursery food.

Whatever its origins, for me it is an all-time classic dish that is soulful, healing, and delicious. Khichiri has huge medicinal value, and is often the first meal to be served after a bout of sickness for it is light and easily digestible, particularly when cooked with ghee which will line the stomach with goodness.

Serves 4

Ingredients:
200g long grain rice
100g mung dal green split lentils – non-split work well too
2 tbsp. ghee
1 cinnamon stick
2 cloves
1 green cardamom pod
1 star anise
4 whole black peppercorns
¼ tsp asafoetida
1 medium onion – finely chopped
2 tsp grated ginger
1 tsp fresh turmeric, grated, or 1 tsp turmeric powder
1 tsp Himalayan salt
1 tsp ground cumin
1 large carrot cubed into ½cm pieces
650ml boiling water
80g fresh spinach, finely chopped
1 tbsp. ghee at the end
Freshly chopped coriander – if preferred

Chef's Tip:

Basmati has a long thin grain and can be too thin to give you the starchiness necessary for this dish; long grain rice is a slightly thicker grain to basmati, if you can get it.

1. Combine the rice and lentils in a bowl, and wash in warm to hand-hot water in a bowl until the water is clear. To do this start by swirling the grains of rice between your fingers in the water. By doing so you will loosen the cloudy starch from the grain and release it into the water. Drain off the water and repeat the process until the water eventually runs clear. This may take several changes of water, but it is worth it, as you reduce the starch content and therefore the calorific value of the rice. Drain and set aside.

2. Melt the ghee in a medium saucepan, and when the ghee is melted and warm add the whole spices: cinnamon stick, cloves, cardamom, star anise and black peppercorns. Sizzle for a few seconds before adding the asafoetida and then the onion. Cook for 3-4 minutes to enable the onions to soften and golden. Now add the ginger, turmeric, salt and cumin, stir gently and allow the spices to cook for 2 minutes on a gentle heat.

3. Add the washed rice, lentils and the carrot, stir in until all the rice/lentils are thoroughly coated in the spices and cook for 2-3 minutes to dry-fry.

4. Now add the water, bring up to temperature i.e. to boiling point, and then drop the temperature to the lowest point and simmer with the lid on tightly for 30 minutes.

5. Check after 20 minutes to ascertain the level of water absorption, stirring gently.

6. When all the water is absorbed turn off the heat and fold in the finely chopped spinach. Replace the lid and let it rest off the heat for 10 minutes. Drizzle with 1 tablespoon of ghee if desired; the consistency should be loose. Garnish with fresh coriander if desired.

Green Garden Peas & Sweetcorn Pilaf Rice

As children we use to love the vibrant colourfulness of this dish and we'd happily eat it on its own with a generous dollop of natural yoghurt, and that's precisely how I've cooked it for my children over the years. Though the vegetables are simple they definitely add flavour and texture to make a simple rice dish more interesting and tasty. I've written about the benefits of ghee in earlier passages; the use of ghee with rice elevates the flavour to a different level.

Serves 4

Ingredients:
200g basmati rice
20g ghee
2 cloves
1 star anise
2 cardamom pods
1 stick of cinnamon
1 tsp cumin seeds
1 onion – thinly sliced
40g peas
40g sweetcorn
¾ tsp salt
380ml boiling water

3-finger pinch of fresh coriander

1. Wash the rice in warm to hand-hot water thoroughly but gently so as not to break the grain and soak in hot water for 30 minutes, time permitting.

2. Melt the ghee in a large pan, and when the ghee is just hot add the cloves, star anise, cardamom pods and cinnamon stick and sizzle for a few seconds before adding the cumin seeds followed by the onion. Stir the onion into the infused oil and whole spices, and cook for a few minutes on a low heat until the onion is softened and turning a light golden brown.

3. Now add the peas, sweetcorn, rice and salt. Coat them well in the oil and stir-fry on a medium heat for about a minute or two until the rice has absorbed any water and is dry-frying.

4. Now add the boiling water, stir well and bring to a simmer, then drop the heat to very low, the lowest point you can get it to.

5. Place a lid on the rice and cook for 10 minutes.

6. Switch off the heat but do not be tempted to lift off the lid. Rest for 10 minutes then finish with the fresh coriander.

7. Enjoy soft fluffy rice.

Peshwari Rice

Peshawari cuisine gets its name from the Peshawar region which is in what is now known as Pakistan. It is an ancient city that has over the years come under the rule of the Mughals, the Sikhs, and the British, giving it a rich culinary tradition and culture. The food of Peshawar is both sweet and savoury all in one. It is a marriage of coconut, raisins, and almonds with ghee or butter, everything that would usually make this a sweet dish but is greatly used with rice and breads, ergo, Peshwari naan. My very simple Peshwari rice recipe yields both great flavour and visual appeal, using the boiling method to cook the rice, infused with whole spices.

Serves 4

Ingredients:
200g basmati rice
1 tsp salt
1 stick of cinnamon
1 star anise
2 green cardamoms
25g sliced almonds
25g golden sultanas
1 tbsp. oil – to fry the onions
50g butter or ghee
1 large onion, finely sliced to fry
Handful of fresh coriander, chopped
Crispy fried onions to garnish – can be shop bought

2 litres of hot water to boil

1. Wash the rice in warm to hand-hot water thoroughly but gently so as not to break the grain and soak in hot water for 30 minutes, time permitting.

2. Strain the rice from the warm water. Place into a pan of hot water (2 litres – there should be at least triple the quantity of water to rice)\ Add the salt, cinnamon sticks, star anise and green cardamoms and bring to the boil, then simmer for 5 minutes or until the rice is 80% cooked.

3. Meanwhile roast the almonds in the oven or toast them in a dry pan, turn them out into a dish and set aside.

4. Place the sultanas in a cup and cover with boiling water to refresh them and make them plump up. Soak for about 5 minutes, drain and set aside.

5. Heat the oil in a frying pan and stir-fry the onions until soft and lightly golden. Lift out of the pan and set aside. Leave the pan aside as you will be using it again. When the rice is cooked, strain the rice out of the boiling water and refresh in cold water to stop the cooking process. Strain in a fine sieve and set aside.

6. Bring the onion pan to the heat, add three quarters of the butter, melt to sizzling, then add the rice, toasted almonds, sultanas, onion and chopped coriander, season with salt and mix through.

7. Grease an ovenproof dish with the remaining butter; transfer the rice to the greased dish. Splash a little water to create steam. Cover in foil to seal and prevent the steam from escaping. Heat in the oven for 20 minutes or until the rice is piping hot.

8. Garnish with pre-fried onions just before serving. Serve with your favourite curry.

Cumin-Fragrant Basmati Rice

This is probably the most simple and commonly cooked rice dish throughout most Indian households and is used to mop up the gravy from the main curry or even accompany the main course for a quick dinner. The addition of the whole spices such as clove in particular is added for its anti-parasitic and digestive properties. Cumin on the other hand is delightfully aromatic and cooling.

Serves 4

Ingredients:
200g basmati rice
½ tbsp. ghee or oil
1 cinnamon stick
3 green cardamoms
3 cloves
1 tsp cumin seeds
1 star anise
350ml warm water
1 tsp salt

1. Wash the rice in warm to hand-hot water in a bowl until the water is clear. To do this start by swirling the grains of rice between your fingers in the water; by doing so you will loosen the cloudy starch from the grain and release it into the water. Drain off the water and repeat the process until the water eventually runs clear. This may take several changes of water, but it is worth it as you reduce the starch content and therefore the calorific value of the rice.

2. Time permitting, soak the rice for 30 minutes in warm water. When ready to use drain the water off the rice.

3. Melt the ghee or oil in a deep pan. Add the cinnamon stick, cardamoms, cloves, cumin seeds and star anise and sizzle for 10 seconds. Now add the rice, boiling water and the salt and stir. Bring to the boil, then reduce the temperature and simmer gently on a very low heat. Cover with a tight lid and cook for 10 minutes. It is important not to remove the lid during cooking.

4. Switch off the heat and let it rest for a further 10 minutes as part of the cooking process before serving.

5. Serve hot with a curry of your choice.

Coconut Rice

I love the subtlety of the coconut in this recipe. It is a delicate flavour, further balanced by the curry leaves and cumin seeds. It works very well with fish dishes, particularly some of the south Indian recipes. It shouldn't be sticky like the Thai variety of coconut rice.

Serves 4

Ingredients:

200g basmati rice, washed and soaked
2 tbsp ghee
1 tsp mustard seeds
1 tsp cumin seeds
1 dried red chilli
5 curry leaves
1 tsp salt
2 tbsp creamed coconut
200ml coconut milk
180ml water
15 roasted cashew nuts and/or peanuts
Pinch of fresh coriander and freshly sliced coconut for garnish
1 fried green chilli to garnish – optional

1. Wash the rice in warm to hand-hot water in a bowl until the water is clear. To do this start by swirling the grains of rice between your fingers in the water; by doing so you will loosen the cloudy starch from the grain and release it into the water. Drain off the water and repeat the process until the water eventually runs clear. This may take several changes of water, but it is worth it, as you reduce the starch content and therefore the calorific value of the rice. Drain in a sieve when ready to use.

2. Heat the ghee in a large saucepan, add the mustard seeds and wait for them to stop popping, before adding the cumin seeds, dried red chilli and curry leaves and the strained rice, then stir-fry for 3-4 minutes.

3. Now add the salt, creamed coconut, coconut milk and water, stir well and bring to the boil. Once at boiling point, place a tight lid on the pan, reduce the temperature to the lowest point possible and cook for 10 minutes. All the water should have been absorbed.

4. Switch off the heat and rest for a further 10 minutes.

5. Now add the roasted cashew nuts, fresh coriander, sliced coconut and crispy pre-fried chilli for garnish.

6. Fork out into a serving bowl and enjoy with a light prawn dish or vegetable curry.

Breads

In every kernel of grain we have everything we need: protein, carbohydrates and fat. Humans have been feasting on grain for over 100,000 years in some primitive form or another. Bread is enormously important in Indian culinary culture. Breads are usually eaten with the main part of the meal. Almost every dish with the exception of kedgeree or biriyani would be accompanied by some type of bread.

There are many different forms of breads starting with the humble chapatti made from wheat flour and rotla usually made from spelt flour, both of which are unleavened breads. Paratha, bhuturas and puri also have an important role at the dinner table. Theplas are more commonly eaten on their own as a snack as they are highly seasoned and very flavoursome.

Most bread in the north and mid-west of India is made from milled wheat flour, called 'atta'. Whilst in south India, where rice and lentils are the main staples, the breads are more like pancakes or crêpes and can be made from a variety of flours including rice flour and lentil flour. These are often fermented as a batter using yoghurt and then cooked like a pancake.

In my family home we mainly eat chapattis, puris, parathas and theplas. I learned to make chapattis at some ridiculous age,

probably knee high to a donkey. The aroma of freshly made breads is quite mesmerizing and I can still recall this wonderful smell perfuming the house and calling me to the kitchen. Nothing has changed really: my children come running through when they can smell the aroma of fresh chapattis, and I struggle to cook them faster than they can eat them!

On a trip to Ahmedabad I had the pleasure of eating romali roti. This is essentially chapatti dough (refined wholemeal flour). It is rolled out tissue thin and cooked on an upturned wok or large frying pan for a less than a minute. It is folded like a large handkerchief to give several layers of beautifully soft bread, peppered with the tiniest bit of butter. **Oh, that first bite was a blissful moment.**

Chapattis or Rotli

Chapattis are a part of everyday Indian life, whether they are in the small thin chapatti form or the slightly thicker roti sometimes called rotli. They are easy to make with four ingredients: flour, water, salt and ghee or oil. They have been exported to many cultures and countries around the globe. In India they are an essential meal component, made freshly at each meal point.

The rolling of chapattis can admittedly take some getting used to. The trick is not to overthink it; let the hand and wrist relax as you are rolling. And don't necessarily look at the board as you roll; in fact closing your eyes until you get the feel for it is often helpful. Let your hands gently move in a rhythm, feeling the bread underneath the rolling pin rather than lifting it off the board to check the evenness of the roll. The more even the roll the better they rise in the cooking process.

Makes 10 small rounds

Ingredients:
2 tbsp. rapeseed oil

200g chapatti flour (preferably wholemeal chapatti flour)

½ tsp salt

3 tbsp. boiling hot water – you may need to add more depending on the density and freshness of flour you are using.

Butter to finish

Equipment:
Thin rolling pin, round rolling board

Flour for dusting

Tawa or metal concave flat pan for toasting

1. Rub the oil into the flour and salt, make a well in the middle and begin to add the water bringing it together into a dough, working quickly to ensure you retain the heat from the water. Rub a little oil into your hands and knead the dough until smooth.

2. Divide into 10 dough balls kneading as you go and dust with flour and roll out into approx 13cm circles.

3. Place on a heated flat tawa; after 30 seconds twist gently to ensure even cooking and turn after 2 minutes when golden brown, then cook on the second side, pressing down gently to allow the air to rise.

4. Remove from the heat when cooked or fully risen.

5. Spread with a sliver of butter to keep the chapattis moist and soften the texture.

6. Enjoy with your main course.

Chef's Tips:

1. Try to buy wholemeal chapatti flour where possible; it gives more elasticity and natural wheat germ and so lowers the glycemic index.

2. Use a spoon if required at first to work the hot water into the flour. Eventually you will need to get your hand in to bring the dough together and work quickly to ensure a soft dough.

Puri

Puri is unleavened deep-fried bread served with the main meal and usually reserved for special occasions, dinner guests or weddings. The dough for puri is made in much the same way as chapattis, but rolled to a small circular disc no more than 7-8cm in diameter, and like a chapatti it will blow up like a balloon in the frying process if rolled evenly. The texture is soft and crisp, depending on the variety, and this can be changed with the use of different proportions of flour. The more regal biscuit like puri, served with a sweet dish such as shrikhand, will be made with semolina flour as well as atta, and the breakfast savoury puri may have a greater proportion of atta (flour) as well as self-raising flour, spices, herbs and seeds.

Puri are quite delicious and I have grown up feasting on the little round creations from childhood. If we were making puri at home I'd immediately ask who was coming for lunch. Today I make them just for fun, and I'll eat them with fresh mango pulp when the Alphonso mangoes are in season.

Serves 4

Ingredients:
200g chapatti flour
50g fine semolina flour – optional
½ tsp salt
½ tsp cumin seeds
¼ tsp black pepper – optional
2 tbsp. ghee (clarified butter)
100ml hand-hot water – you may not require all of this

Oil for deep-frying

You can also add other seasonings to this mixture like turmeric, green chillies and bishop's weed (ajwain) to make a more savoury puri, which can just be enjoyed on its own.

Equipment:
Thin rolling pin, round rolling board
Oil vessel for frying puri

1. Combine the two flours together and place in a deep bowl together with the salt, cumin seeds, black pepper and ghee. Rub the ghee into the flour and gently add the water, little by little, but work quickly to ensure you retain the heat from the water in the flour – hold some water back and use as necessary to knead into the dough. Dip your fingers into a little oil, rub over your hands and knead the dough for about 2 minutes to get a smooth silken finish; the dough should be warm and soft. Cover the dough with a plate and allow it to rest for 20 minutes.

2. Tear the dough into little dough balls about the size of a walnut.

3. Using a flat rolling board and a thin rolling pin, roll out to a 2.5 inch diameter and ¼cm thickness, ensuring that the puri is even on all sides. (Alternatively roll out into one big puri and use a cutter to cut to the right size.)

4. Heat the oil to deep-fry the puris. Using a slotted metal spoon, remove the puris from the oil when medium/suntan brown and place onto absorbent papers.

Methi Theplas

Theplas originate from the Gujarat region of India. They are made from a combination of whole wheat flour and chickpea flour and contain fresh fenugreek leaves as well as herbs and spices. The recipe for theplas can vary from town to town or indeed home to home and others may also make them with a finely chopped spinach filling as an alternative to the fresh fenugreek. I stay loyal to my grandmother's recipe, using only fresh fenugreeks as the vegetable and loads of it. Even the mere mention of them makes my mouth water. I could eat these at any time of the day. They are the perfect type of food, bread in form, spicy, piquant, slightly bitter from the fresh fenugreek, and very lightly fried off, just all the hallmarks of a perfect bit of food.

Serves 4

Ingredients:
6 tbsp. finely chopped fresh methi (fenugreek) leaves
120g whole wheat chapatti flour
60g gram flour (chickpea flour)
½ tsp green chilli, finely chopped
1 tsp ground roasted cumin
2 tsp finely chopped ginger
½ tsp turmeric powder
1 tsp salt
2 tbsp. oil
2 tbsp. full fat yoghurt
1 tbsp. sesame seeds

Oil to griddle/bake the theplas

1. Separate the leaves from the stalks of the methi, discard the stalks and then wash the methi, dry with a paper towel and chop very finely. Set aside.

2. In a large bowl, add the two flours along with the green chilli, cumin, ginger, turmeric and salt and mix well to ensure an even distribution of the spices. Add the oil and the yoghurt and rub into the flour, binding everything together.

3. Now add the methi leaves and sesame seeds and bind together again. You may need a little hot water but don't be tempted to add too much. Use your hands to bring the dough together and knead for a few minutes.

4. If the dough is getting sticky in the kneading process, add a little more flour and knead again.

5. Rub a little oil over your hands to knead once more to give a silken texture to the finished dough – you should have some elasticity in the dough. Cover and rest for 30 minutes.

6. Make medium-size balls of the dough – slightly larger than a golf ball – and roll it to a disc of 5 inches in diameter, dusting in wheat flour in between rolls if necessary.

7. Heat a thick tawa, place the rolled thepla on the tawa and let it cook slightly on one side, for about a minute on a low heat. Turn it over to the other side, apply 1 teaspoon of oil or ghee and cook for about 90 seconds and then turn once more back to the original side again and apply a tiny amount of oil until it's cooked and has formed little brown toasting spots.

8. Repeat with the rest of the theplas in the same way and stack them in a warm place or steel tin to retain their softness.

Naan in a Pan!

Naan bread first appeared in the royal courts in Delhi around the 1400s though it is said to have originally come from the ports of Egypt much earlier than that (essentially the importation of yeast came to India from Egypt and with it the recipe for naan). It takes its name from the Persian word for bread 'non'. This recipe makes light and fluffy naan breads with very little fuss. Leave as long as possible for the proving stage if you can; it will definitely give you compliments as the yoghurt and ghee work their way into the flour, giving depth of flavour.

Makes 4

Ingredients:
250g strong white bread flour (plus extra for dusting)
¾ tsp caster sugar
1 tsp fine salt
4g fast acting yeast
1 tsp roasted cumin seeds
2½ tbsp. natural yoghurt
1 tbsp. of ghee or melted butter (cooled) + extra for brushing
100ml lukewarm milk
Oil for oiling bowl and baking sheets
½ tsp onion seeds or caraway seeds
Ghee or butter for brushing
Fresh coriander leaves

1. In a large mixing bowl, mix together the flour, sugar, salt, yeast and cumin seeds. Make a well in the centre and add the yoghurt and the melted ghee/butter. Mix together, then gradually add the milk and knead to make a soft sticky dough. Add a little water if the dough seems dry. Tip the dough out onto a lightly floured surface and knead for about 5 minutes until you have a soft smooth dough. Put in a large, lightly oiled bowl, turning the dough until coated in oil. Cover with lightly oiled cling film and leave in a warm place until doubled in size (about 30 minutes).

2. Once the dough has doubled in size, tip it out onto a lightly floured surface and punch it down, then divide it into 4 balls. Set them on a floured baking sheet, sprinkle lightly with flour, cover them loosely with cling film and leave for 20 minutes.

3. Flatten the balls with your hands or a rolling pin into teardrops or ovals. Put the prepared naans on floured baking sheets. Place a non-stick frying pan over a very high heat until it is really hot. Put a naan in the pan. When it starts to bubble and go brown turn it over and cook the other side. Keep turning it over until it is cooked through, puffed up and scorched here and there.

4. Brush with ghee or melted butter and sprinkle with onion seeds or caraway seeds. Cover and keep warm until you have finished cooking the rest of the naans. Alternatively the naans can be cooked in the oven. Heat the oven to its highest setting. Roll out the naans and place on a very lightly oiled baking sheet, brush with melted ghee and sprinkle with onion or caraway seeds. Cook for 15-20 minutes, or until browned and puffed up.

5. Garnish with fresh coriander leaves and serve.

Chef's Tip:

Add some chopped garlic with the ghee before cooking for garlic naans.

Plain Parathas

When I was growing up, parathas were a staple in my household. They are essentially unleavened Indian flat breads that are much thinner than naan and thicker than chapattis. They are a step up from chapattis, I'd say, and use more ghee or oil since they have to be rolled, buttered (or oiled) and then re-rolled three or four times over to layer in the crispiness and butteriness, that makes them similar to puff pastry. Though stuffed parathas are delicious, I prefer the plain ones when accompanying a main meal. I prefer to keep the spices and flavours in their correct places when eating food together.

Serves 4

Ingredients:
200g chapatti flour
3.5 tbsp. oil
½ tsp salt
100ml tepid water – 47˚C

Extra flour for dusting whilst rolling – in a bowl
Flat pan – tawa – similar to one used for making pancakes

1. Place the flour, oil and salt in a bowl and mix well. Add the water a little at a time (in case the flour density/grade varies) and knead for 2-3 minutes until the dough ball comes away from the bowl. Take a drop of oil and rub into the hands and knead again to give it a smooth and silken finish. Work quickly to ensure the dough doesn't cool down too much and toughen up in the process.

2. Divide the dough into 10 balls, each roughly weighing around 30g. Roll each piece of dough between your palms forming a ball and then press the ball between your palms to flatten, creating a disc shape. Take one disc of dough, make sure to cover the rest so they don't dry out, and press both sides into the bowl of extra flour for dusting.

3. Then roll out the disc into about a 10cm circle. Spread a ¼ tsp of oil onto the surface and sprinkle a pinch of flour over the oil. Fold the round into quarters and then roll back into a disc.

4. Dip the disc back into the flour and roll out into a 12cm round. Dip back into the flour if the paratha starts to stick to the surface as you're rolling. Repeat once more, to create the layers in the paratha which give parathas their uniqueness.

5. Now heat the tawa over a medium low heat. Transfer the rolled out paratha to the pan. Cook until you see bubbles forming. Flip the paratha over using a spatula. Drizzle ½ teaspoon of oil onto the side that was just cooked and spread the oil around with your spatula. Cook for about 1 minute on a low heat. You will see more bubbles forming and you can check to make sure the paratha is ready to flip by lifting a side of the paratha and peeking underneath. If you see a few reddish brown spots beginning to form, it's ready.

6. Turn the heat up to high and flip the paratha one more time. This time, press onto the paratha with your spatula for about 30 to 40 seconds. This will help it puff up, then remove from the tawa, place on a plate that is lined with greaseproof paper or a tissue and cover with a tea towel until ready to serve. Repeat with the remaining dough balls, rolling out whilst you're waiting for the parathas to cook.

Sweets & Puddings

Sadly desserts are often the point at which many people choose to part company with Indian food as they are often perceived as too cloyingly sweet for the Western palate. So bearing in mind that this cook book will be used (although not exclusively) by European cooks, I'm tearing up the rule book!

Although you will find included in this chapter familiar Indian dishes such as kulfi (albeit with a twist!) or shrikand, I have also fused the flavours found in traditional Indian foods with popular European style desserts.

Similarly fruits such as berries, although not represented in Indian cuisine, are readily available to the Western cook and as such have been included in some of the dishes along with fruits such as figs, mangoes and limes that are indigenous to Indian cuisine. Such fruits are strongly reminiscent of Indian food and help to cut through the savoury flavours from the previous courses.

You'll find many of my dessert recipes include yoghurt as a major ingredient. Yoghurt is to Indian cuisine as cream is to European cooking. It plays an enormous part in Indian culinary life.

Historically speaking yoghurt is seen as a very self-sufficient ingredient in rural India as many villagers will have access to a communal herd of cattle and hence their milk, which is then used in many different ways to make other ingredients such as ghee, yoghurt and cheese.

I hope you enjoy experimenting with both the timeless classics and the modern fusion recipes in this chapter.

Baked Figs with Creamy Yoghurt

Figs are considered the fruit of the gods in many cultures, and they are abundantly available throughout India. When they are in season they are beautifully ripe and syrupy, the kind of fruit that lends itself to a wonderful molasses. The pairing with cinnamon and nutmeg is heavenly and this delightful dish is finished off with creamy baked yoghurt and toasted almonds.

Serves 4

Ingredients:
8 figs cut into quarters
50g butter plus extra for greasing
2 tbsp. brown sugar
2 tsp pomegranate molasses syrup
1 tsp ground cinnamon
1 tsp ground nutmeg
5 tbsp. runny honey
Full fat Greek yoghurt to serve
Sliced almonds – toasted

1. Preheat the oven to gas mark 4/180°C.

2. Grease the bottom of your baking dish with a little butter. Place the quartered figs on the dish and dot the butter on top.

3. Sprinkle the sugar, pomegranate molasses, cinnamon and nutmeg over the figs and bake in the oven for 15 minutes.

4. Remove from the oven, drizzle with the honey and bake for a further 10 minutes.

5. Meanwhile divide the yoghurt into the serving bowls.

6. Remove the figs from the oven and divide into the bowls with the yoghurt.

7. Sprinkle with the sliced toasted almonds.

8. Enjoy!

Mango & Lime Coconut Fool

I have taken a bit of poetic licence here and added my Indian twist to the classic British fruit and cream dessert. I hope you will agree that the combination of mango and coconut is a marriage made in heaven. The Indian flavour profiles work perfectly with the creamy texture of the fool. This is lovely when eaten on a warm day, being light with a balance of sweet and tart fruit flavours, and is therefore a perfect dessert to follow a rich meal.

Serves 4

Ingredients:
2 tbsp. coconut flakes
2 ripe mangoes
300g thick full fat natural yoghurt or curd cheese
Zest and juice of 1 lime
2 passion fruit – flesh scooped out
Fresh mint leaves for garnish
Mango slices for garnish

1. Dry toast the coconut flakes on a low heat in a non-stick pan for a few minutes until lightly golden brown. Set aside.

2. Remove the flesh from the mangoes and puree the fruit in a food processor until smooth.

3. Place the yoghurt, lime juice, zest and mango puree in a bowl and stir through lightly.

4. Decant into serving bowls or glasses.

5. Spoon on the passion fruit seeds and juice and garnish with the mint leaves, coconut flakes and mango slices.

6. Place in the fridge for a few hours or until ready to serve.

7. Enjoy this delicious dessert guilt-free knowing that it's full of superfoods and nothing else.

Chef's Tips:

1. *This is a super dessert to make ahead if you are entertaining. It is also excellent for lower calorie sinless deliciousness!*

2. *Add a cheeky dash of mascarpone cheese with the Greek yoghurt if you want the dessert to be a little creamier.*

3. *Mangoes are packed with vitamin B6 which is good for brain health.*

Plums with Ginger, Cinnamon & Mascarpone Cheese

Plums are a delightful fruit and having had plum trees for years it seemed only right that I create something particularly delicious with them, and so I've paired them with the smallest amount of ginger and cinnamon then topped with mascarpone cheese to create the most blissful union. I hope you agree.

Serves 4

Ingredients:

100g bulgur wheat – soaked in cold water and drained (or you could use quinoa or whole rolled oats)

Butter to grease the tray

400g plums, cut in half and de-stoned

1 inch knob of stem ginger, finely sliced into julienne

50ml honey or 50g brown sugar

1 tsp ground cinnamon

½ tsp ground nutmeg

75g diced butter

500g mascarpone cheese

50g brown sugar with a ½ tsp of cinnamon mixed through it.

300ml double cream

3 tbsp. mascarpone cheese

1 tbsp. sliced almonds – toasted

Cinnamon to dust

Mint leaves to garnish

Extra cream or ice cream (optional)

1. Preheat the oven to 200°C/gas mark 6.

2. Soak the bulgur wheat in cold water for 15 minutes, drain and squeeze out as much water as possible. Set aside.

3. Gently toast the sliced almonds and set aside.

4. Grease a large ovenproof tray, place the plums in the tray and scatter over the ginger and honey or sugar.

5. Add the cinnamon and nutmeg to the bulgur wheat and mix well. Melt the butter in a pan. Scatter the bulgur wheat over the plums and pour over the melted butter.

6. Place in the oven for 15 minutes.

7. Remove from the oven and spoon on the 500g of mascarpone cheese; spread it evenly over the plums and then top with the brown sugar mixed with the cinnamon.

8. Place in the oven once more for 15 to 20 minutes or until golden brown.

9. Remove from the oven, and allow to cool and then place in the fridge for an hour or two until ready to serve.

10. While the plums are cooling whip the cream until it is just holding its shape and stir through 3 tablespoons of mascarpone until smooth.

11. Attach a plain nozzle to a piping bag and fill with the cream and mascarpone mixture. Remove the plums from the fridge and pipe small blobs of cream over the top of the plums.

12. Garnish with the toasted almonds and a dusting of cinnamon. Serve with a little mint to the side and some extra cream if desired or ice cream!

Chocolate & Ginger Mousse with Ginger & Mango Chocolate Bark

This is a great dessert to make ahead for a dinner party as all the elements can be prepared in advance. Chocolate and ginger work so well together and the chocolate bark really gives this dish the wow factor!

Serves 4

Ingredients:

150g good quality dark chocolate, at least 70% cocoa solids, broken into small pieces

30g butter

1 tbsp. golden syrup

6 free-range medium eggs

3 tsp ginger juice from 8cm finely grated fresh root ginger

For the chocolate bark:

100g good quality dark chocolate, at least 70% cocoa solids, broken into small pieces

8-10 pieces of crystallised ginger

Small handful of dried mango pieces

Gold edible glitter

1. Put the chocolate, butter and golden syrup into a heatproof bowl over a small saucepan of simmering water (make sure that the bowl doesn't touch the water) and warm over a medium heat until melted.

2. Meanwhile, separate the eggs, putting the whites into a clean, grease-free bowl and the yolks into another. Set aside.

3. Place a sieve over the bowl of egg yolks. Hold the grated ginger in your hand over the sieve and squeeze the juice from it (you should get about 3 teaspoonsful). Stir the juice into the yolks.

4. When the chocolate, golden syrup and butter have melted, let the mixture cool slightly and then pour it slowly into the yolk mixture, stirring constantly until smooth.

5. Whisk the egg whites until they form soft peaks – try not to overwhisk them, or the mousse will become too stiff. When they are ready, gently but thoroughly fold them into the chocolate mixture so that they are completely combined.

6. Pour the mousse into small cups, ramekins or shallow serving dishes and place in the freezer for 20 minutes to chill, or transfer to the fridge if not eating them straight away.

7. For the chocolate bark: Line a baking tray with baking paper. Melt the chocolate in a heatproof bowl over a pan of simmering water.

8. Spread the dark chocolate in a thin, even layer on the baking paper. Scatter over the crystallised ginger and mango pieces and sprinkle with the edible glitter. Place in the fridge to set.

9. When the chocolate has set, whizz half of it in a food processor to make rough crumbs. Using a sharp knife cut the remaining half of chocolate on the tray into triangular shaped shards. Serve the chocolate mousse sprinkled with the chocolate crumbs and topped with shards of the chocolate bark.

Nutritional Tip:

Dark chocolate contains anthocyanins, which help regulate blood flow, and is also a good source of magnesium, which boosts energy levels.

Lime, Cardamom & Coconut Cheesecakes

These little desserts are always popular in our cookery classes and really take very little time to make. The combination of ginger, lime and coconut is a winner and the cheesecakes look very pretty when garnished with a sprinkling of toasted coconut and a slice of lime.

Makes 6 individual cheesecakes

Ingredients:

For the base:
150g ginger biscuits, crushed
75g butter, melted
½ tsp ground cardamom

For the cheesecake mixture:
2 x 250g tubs mascarpone cheese
40g icing sugar
Finely grated zest and juice of 2 limes
3 tbsp. very finely grated coconut cream (from a block)
Sliced limes to garnish or extra zest

For the toasted coconut:
Handful of dried coconut flakes

1. Firstly make the base. Pulse the biscuits in the food processor into crumbs. Melt the butter, stir in the crushed biscuits and the ground cardamom. Leave to cool slightly then divide between six small dishes and press down firmly. Chill in the fridge until needed.

2. Now make the cheesecake mixture. Beat the mascarpone cheese, icing sugar, lime zest and juice and finely grated coconut cream. Pour or spoon the mixture onto the chilled bases and spread evenly. Place in the fridge to set.

3. For the toasted coconut place the coconut flakes in a pan over a medium heat until they are mostly golden brown. Take off the heat and continue to cook in the residual heat of the pan until they are all golden brown. Turn out onto a plate to cool completely.

4. When the cheesecakes are set remove them from the fridge and garnish with the toasted coconut and remaining lime zest and slices of lime.

Spiced Caramelized Pears with Whipped Ginger Cream

For a dish that looks and tastes so delicious, you wouldn't imagine that it takes just 15 minutes all-in to prepare it and even less time to devour it! This recipe is a crowd pleaser, using simple ingredients to tickle your taste buds. If you're not big on stem ginger cream, try serving it with Madagascan vanilla ice cream.

Serves 4

Ingredients:

For the whipped ginger cream:
150ml double cream
1 tbsp. syrup from the stem ginger
2 pieces of stem ginger, finely chopped

For the pears:
50g butter
3 dessert pears, peeled, cored and cut into thick, even slices
60g brown sugar
¼ tsp ground cinnamon
⅛ tsp clove powder
¼ tsp cardamom powder
40g walnuts, halved
Chilli powder for dusting

1. Start by whipping the cream until it forms soft peaks that only just hold their shape. Add the syrup and re-beat just enough to blend in. (Do not overbeat the cream as it can curdle easily). Now fold in the stem ginger and set aside in a cool place until ready to serve.

2. Using a large non-stick frying pan, melt the butter and add the pears, sugar, cinnamon, clove powder and cardamom powder. Cook for about 5-6 minutes on a medium heat.

3. Add the walnuts and cook for a further 2 minutes.

4. Now increase the heat and cook for 6-8 minutes on a slightly higher temperature until the pears are golden brown and have a sticky caramelized glaze.

5. Plate up and serve with a dollop of the ginger cream or ice cream.

6. Garnish with a light dusting of chilli powder on top.

7. Enjoy!

Chocolate & Chilli Tart with Cardamom, Pistachios & Raspberries

This tart is super rich with tantalizing hints of chilli and cardamom. For a dessert that looks and tastes so amazing this is surprisingly easy to make – even the chocolate pastry is a doddle. Dot a few fresh raspberries over the top to offset the sweetness and dive into chocolate heaven!

Serves 10-12

Ingredients:
225g (8oz) plain flour
125g (4½oz) butter
25g (1oz) cocoa powder
2 tbsp. light muscovado sugar
1 egg yolk, beaten
3 tbsp. cold water
3 medium eggs, lightly whisked
450ml (16 fl oz) double cream
200g (7oz) 70% dark chocolate, broken into small pieces
100g (3½oz) milk chocolate, broken into small pieces
½ tsp chilli powder
10 cardamom pods – husks discarded, seeds crushed in a pestle and mortar

For the garnish:
Handful of pistachio nuts, some chopped, some left whole
Handful of fresh raspberries, some halved, some left whole

Crème fraîche and chilli flakes, to serve

1. Put the flour in a large bowl and rub in the butter until it resembles fine breadcrumbs, then stir in the cocoa powder and sugar. Mix the egg yolk with the water and add to the mixture. Mix with a round bladed knife until the dough comes together. Wrap the pastry in cling film and rest it in the fridge for 30 minutes.

2. Once the dough has rested roll it out to the thickness of a pound coin and use to line a 23cm (9in) fluted flan ring. Chill again for at least 30 minutes. Preheat the oven to 190°C/fan 170°C/gas 5. Place the flan ring on a baking tray, line the pastry with baking parchment and fill with baking beans and bake for 10-15 minutes or until the pastry starts to lose its sheen. Remove from the oven and cool. Reduce the oven temperature to 170°C/fan 150°C/gas 3.

3. Lightly whisk the eggs and set aside.

4. Meanwhile, heat the cream in a pan to just below boiling (if it boils allow it to cool for 5 minutes). Add the chocolate gradually and whisk until smooth and melted. Gradually beat in the 3 eggs, chilli powder and the crushed cardamom seeds. Pour into the tart case and bake for 25-30 minutes or until just set, but still slightly wobbly in the middle. Cool completely.

5. When the tart has cooled, top with the pistachios and raspberries.

6. Slice the tart and serve with a dollop of crème fraîche sprinkled with chilli flakes.

Passionfruit & Cardamom Panna Cotta

The zingy flavour of the passionfruit jelly is the crowning glory in this silky dessert. Infusing the panna cotta with cardamom helps to cut through the creaminess of this indulgent dish. This is another great pud that can be made ahead of time in its entirety.

Serves 4

Ingredients:

For the jelly:
100ml passionfruit juice
20g golden caster sugar
1 sheet of leaf gelatine (bronze)

For the panna cotta:
1 tsp vegetable oil to grease
600ml double cream
3 green cardamoms, lightly bruised
1 pared strip lemon zest
60g caster sugar
1 tsp vanilla paste
3 sheets leaf gelatine

Equipment:
4 x 150ml dariole moulds

1. Brush the dariole moulds very lightly with the vegetable oil and invert onto a wire rack to drain.

2. For the jelly: Heat the passionfruit juice and sugar in a saucepan, stirring until the sugar has completely dissolved. Meanwhile put the sheet of gelatine into cold water and leave to soak for 5 minutes to soften.

3. Take the juice off the heat, squeeze out the gelatine and add it to the juice. Stir until the gelatine melts completely.

4. Pour an equal amount of the jelly mixture into each of the dariole moulds. Chill in the refrigerator for 1 hour or until firmly set.

5. For the panna cotta: Put the cream into a saucepan with the bruised cardamom pods (lightly crush the cardamom pods with the side of a knife) and lemon zest, then bring to scalding point over a medium heat.

6. Remove from the heat, add the sugar and stir to dissolve. Set the panna cotta mixture aside for 20 minutes.

7. Meanwhile soak the 3 gelatine leaves in cold water for 5 minutes to soften.

8. Remove the lemon zest and cardamom pods from the infused cream. Add the vanilla paste and gently reheat over a low to medium heat.

9. Squeeze the excess water from the gelatine and add the gelatine sheets to the warmed cream, stirring to dissolve. Strain the mixture through a sieve into a jug and pour the cream into the dariole moulds. Refrigerate for 3 hours until set or overnight.

10. To unmould the panna cottas dip the moulds in hot water for no more than 5 seconds, invert onto a serving plate and whilst holding the mould to the plate give a sideways shake to release the panna cotta. For a lovely textural contrast, serve with the lime and coconut shortbread biscuits on the next page.

Lime & Coconut Shortbread

This is my take on the somewhat traditional nankhatai biscuits that I grew up with. They were always a little bit too sweet for my liking so I have brought together two of my favourite biscuits in one place. The lime zest in this recipe offsets the sweetness and the coconut adds a lovely textural element to this scrumptious hybrid.

Makes 18-20 biscuits

Ingredients:
100g unsalted butter, at room temperature, cut into small cubes
50g caster sugar
½ tsp vanilla extract
150g plain flour, sifted, plus extra for dusting
5 tbsp. desiccated coconut, 4 tbsp. for the shortbread dough, 1 tbsp. for sprinkling
1 lime, zested
Granulated sugar for sprinkling

1. Preheat the oven to 160°C/gas mark 3.

2. In a dry frying pan toast the desiccated coconut until it turns golden brown, then remove from the pan and set aside to cool.

3. Zest the lime and set aside.

4. Mix together the butter and sugar, using an electric hand whisk, until pale and smooth. Add the vanilla extract, then gently mix in the flour until completely incorporated (try not to work the flour too much or the biscuits will not be so crumbly). Add 4 tablespoons of the toasted desiccated coconut and all of the lime zest. Using your hands, squeeze the mixture together into a ball of dough.

5. Gently roll the dough out to about 5mm/¼ inch thick (dust the work surface with a little flour if the dough sticks). Cut into shapes using a biscuit cutter. Transfer the biscuits to a baking tray lined with baking parchment (or a non-stick baking tray) and chill in the fridge for 15 minutes to rest (chilling makes them hold their shape better when baking).

6. Before cooking, sprinkle each biscuit with a pinch of granulated sugar. Bake in the preheated oven for 15-20 minutes, or until pale golden brown.

7. Remove from the oven, sprinkle with the reserved 1 tablespoon of toasted coconut and transfer the biscuits to a wire rack to cool.

Mumbai Mess

I've always been a big fan of Eton Mess, though I always find the proportion of fruit to be a bit lacking and occasionally the choice of fruit to be a tad too tart. So in making my own version with an Indian twist I've used all my favourite exotic fruits.

This is such a great time saving dessert. Make your meringue ahead of time and assemble all the components just before you are ready to serve. This looks so elegant piled up in pretty glasses or glass bowls finished with a sprig of mint. If you're short on time use shop bought meringues (I won't tell if you won't!).

Serves 6

Ingredients:
3 large egg whites
175g golden caster sugar
1 mango, diced
1 papaya, diced
2 passionfruit, pulp spooned out

For the mango coulis:
325g fresh mango, cubed
1 teaspoon icing sugar or more to taste

600ml double cream
Sprigs of mint to garnish

You will also need a baking tray measuring 11 x 16 inches (28 x 40 cm), lined with non-stick silicone paper (parchment).

1. Preheat the oven to 150°C/gas mark 2.

2. Place the egg whites into a clean, grease-free bowl and whisk them until they form stiff peaks. Add the caster sugar, 1 tablespoon at a time, and continue to whisk until each tablespoon of sugar has been thoroughly incorporated.

3. Now take rounded dessertspoonfuls of the mixture and place them in rows on the lined baking tray. Place the baking tray in the oven on the centre shelf, turn the heat down to 140°C/gas mark 1 and cook the meringues for 1 hour. After that, turn the oven off and leave the meringues in the oven to dry out overnight, or until the oven is completely cold.

4. Meanwhile dice the mango and papaya and scoop the pulp from the passionfruit and set aside. For the coulis whizz the 325g of fresh mango with a teaspoon of icing sugar until you have a smooth puree.

5. When you're ready to assemble the dessert, whip the double cream until it is just holding its shape.

6. Now break up the meringues into roughly 1 inch (2.5cm) pieces, place them in a large mixing bowl, add the chopped fruit, then gently fold in the whipped cream.

7. Now gently fold in all but about 2 tablespoons of the coulis to give a marbled effect.

8. Divide the mixture between the serving bowls, spoon over the passionfruit pulp, drizzle over the remaining coulis and garnish with a sprig of mint. Serve immediately.

Lime Possets with Mango & Mint Salad

I absolutely adore lemon posset, which has been enjoying something of a renaissance recently. However I wanted to put my Indian twist on this classic favourite and so came up with this delicious fresh concoction of lime, mango and mint. This really is a super quick dessert to make but so tasty that your guests will think you've been slaving away in the kitchen for hours. Just smile sweetly and graciously accept all the compliments that flow your way!

Serves 6

Ingredients:

For the posset:
500ml double cream
Juice and zest of 5 limes
150g golden caster sugar
1 tsp vanilla essence

For the mango and mint salad:
1 large mango, peeled and cut into slices
6 large mint leaves, finely sliced
Small sprigs of mint to garnish

1. Firstly make the posset. Put the cream, caster sugar and vanilla essence in a pan and bring to the boil, stirring occasionally to dissolve the sugar. Lower the heat and leave to simmer for a few minutes, stirring from time to time. Whisk in the lime juice and zest and remove from the heat.

2. Sieve the hot cream into 6 glasses and chill in the fridge.

3. Top each of the possets with the sliced mango and sprinkle the finely sliced mint over the top. Garnish each posset with a small sprig of mint.

Shrikand

This is a delicious creamy dessert traditionally made with curd cheese and then flavoured with saffron and cardamom or pistachios and mango. Shrikand was always the sweet dish served at weddings with semolina puris; in fact it was so sweet that I used to focus on the puri with just the tiniest smear of shrikand! It is for this reason that I have taken down the sugar levels a few notches and my take on this dish is a delicate balance of creamy, sweet and savoury. This is best served in shot glasses or martini glasses.

Serves 4

Ingredients:
1 pinch saffron soaked in 5ml hot water
400g mascarpone cheese
100g full fat Greek yoghurt
60g caster sugar
¼ tsp ground cardamom
2 tbsp. sliced pistachio nuts
¼ pomegranate – deseeded

A few pistachio nuts held back to garnish
A few pomegranate seeds held back to garnish
Edible rose petals to garnish

1. In a small cup add the hot water and saffron – allow this to infuse for 5 minutes.

2. Meanwhile combine the mascarpone, yoghurt and sugar in a bowl and beat together until the sugar has dissolved.

3. Now add the cardamom, pistachio nuts, ¾ of the pomegranate seeds and drained saffron and fold into the yoghurt mix.

4. Allow to chill for 2 hours or as long as possible.

5. To serve, spoon into glasses and garnish with the pistachio nuts, remaining pomegranate seeds and edible rose petals.

6. Enjoy!

CHEF'S TIP:
Swap the mascarpone for probiotic yoghurt to increase the nutritional value; do make sure you use full fat yoghurt (10%).

Drinks
& Juices

Drinks are an essential part of Indian daily life from a heat and hydration point of view as well as a social perspective. As the population go about their business, the intense heat can be punishingly hard and so drinks are designed to be hydrating, cooling and refreshing pick-me-ups for different seasons and climates. Drinks vendors of all kinds can be found on every bustling street corner, even just walking through the street selling to passers-by much like you might find on any beach in Spain. Chai-walas, meaning tea vendors, can be heard making their call for tea 'chai wala – chai garam', the most important drink in all of India.

Alcohols such as wine and beers have not traditionally played a major role due to prohibition on religious grounds in certain parts of India, though there has always been a somewhat underground drinking culture throughout the centuries. For the most part drinks have consisted of teas, fruit juices and sodas, including drinks of the Coca-Cola and Pepsi kind that are major brands in India too.

As the day goes on different drinks will become available and nothing quite quenches a thirst like a limbo ki pani, a lime water cooler, or shirdi ki ras meaning sugar cane juice, both of which can be intensely sweet but pick you up and refresh you for sure.

Drinks are also very seasonal and so fruit juices will vary thorough the year and in this chapter you will find a wide variety of drinks for each season and palate. Don't worry; I've adjusted my recipes to contain a lower sugar content to suit our Western tastes.

Masala Chai
'Chai Wala – Chai Garam'

'Chai Wala Chai Garam' is an expression that holds great memories of India and of my father calling out 'Chai Wala Chai Garam' most tea times; it was his way of remembering his childhood with fondness.

Chai is the Indian word for tea, one of the most important drinks or refreshments in India – usually drunk in the morning and in the mid-afternoon. In India it is customary to be offered a beverage of a sort upon one's arrival at someone's home and is expressed as 'chai pani', which literally means tea or water. Tea is a welcome refreshing drink in India and is 'cooked', or rather boiled, you've guessed... with spices!

Of course, the offer of chai extends to any cold drink or sherbet, as it is often referred to, which means a cool drink. These days you're just as likely to be offered a Pepsi... in a bottle of course.

Serves 4

Ingredients:
300ml water
1 tbsp. of Indian tea leaves, Assam teas, Lipton or English breakfast tea
2 bruised cardamom pods
¼ tsp chai masala (see the Spice Blends chapter for this spice blend)
200ml of milk
Sugar to taste

1. Pour the water into a saucepan and as the water begins to boil add the loose leaf tea, the cardamom pods and the chai masala; stir and bring to the boil. Let it simmer for 1 minute on a low temperature.

2. Add the milk and stir once again, bring to the boil, add the sugar if using, then stir and hold on a simmer for 2 minutes to brew the tea.

3. Finally bring the tea back to the boil. Switch off the heat and strain through a tea strainer or a small fine sieve. Pour into the cups and enjoy with an Indian snack.

Adduwali Chai

Adduwali chai is simply tea with freshly grated ginger. It is a favourite pick-me-up and is a spicy version of the traditional Indian tea. Here the tea leaves are actually brewed with the freshly grated ginger and then the milk and sugar is added. Once again sugar is optional.

Ginger tea is great for a sore throat or headache induced by blocked sinuses. I always keep a block of ginger by my teapots, whether I'm making chai in the full Indian style or just grating the ginger into a cup of regular English breakfast tea.

Serves 2

Ingredients:
2 cups of water
1 inch piece of ginger, grated
1 teabag of your favourite brand, or
2 tsp of loose leaf tea
1 cup of milk
Sugar to taste

1. Pour the water into a saucepan and as the water begins to boil add the loose leaf tea, and the ginger, stir and bring to the boil. Let it simmer for 1 minute on a low temperature.

2. Add the milk and stir once again, bring to the boil, add the sugar if using, stir and hold on a simmer for 2 minutes to brew the tea.

3. Finally bring the tea back to the boil. Switch off the heat and strain through a tea strainer or a small fine sieve. Pour into the cups and enjoy with an Indian snack.

Turmeric Latte

Sometimes referred to as 'golden milk', turmeric latte has acquired a cult following in recent years, 'golden milk' being one of the top online searches associated with turmeric. There is a huge surge of interest in this drink – another sign that the Indian subcontinent may be ahead of the hipster curve. Turmeric has been enjoying some rightful recognition in recent times for its many health-giving benefits, some of which I myself have relied upon from time to time.

In Indian culinary use turmeric is revered for its natural antibiotic, digestive, antibacterial and anti-inflammatory properties. I've grown up drinking what I refer to as my medicinal cocoa so I consider myself an authority on turmeric milk, and can vouch for its healing properties.

Serves 1

Ingredients:
250ml semi-skimmed milk
½ tsp turmeric powder
¼ tsp ground pepper
3-4 strands of saffron
2 tsp honey

1. Add the milk, turmeric, pepper and saffron into a milk pot and bring to a boil on a low flame. It is important to keep it on a low flame to infuse the spices into the milk.

2. Once the milk is simmering, stir in the honey.

3. Increase the flame to bring it to a fast boil and switch off.

4. Strain the milk into a mug and enjoy while it is hot!

Chef's Tips:

1. *The pepper can be replaced with a ¼ teaspoon of cinnamon powder for a soothing wintry beverage.*

2. *Almond milk can be used instead of cow's milk for a nutty variation or if you are not keen on regular milk.*

Lassi

Lassi is a cooling yoghurt drink. I prefer the savoury and simple version because I find it most refreshing, particularly in the summer or in a hot climate such as India. The yoghurt laced with coarsely ground roasted cumin, a dash of salt and refreshing mint is all it needs in the first instance. If you then want to embellish it with a tarka with curry leaves and mustard seeds that's just a bonus. The mustard seeds drop to the bottom but the refreshing mint and curry leaves float up to the top. I also prefer the water to yoghurt ratio to remain fairly high to keep the light and hydrating element to it. I particularly love it with a good biriyani.

The sweet variety of lassi, often made with mangoes, is in my opinion a dessert masquerading as a drink so I would almost put that into the smoothie category.

Serves 4

Ingredients:
500g plain yoghurt
300ml cold water
¼ tsp Himalayan salt
¼ tsp sugar
1 tsp roughly ground roasted cumin

For the tarka:
1 tsp rapeseed oil
⅛ tsp black mustard seeds
8 curry leaves

8 mint leaves – roughly chopped
8 chunks of ice

1. Place the yoghurt in a bowl, add half of the water and whisk until light and frothy. Slowly add the rest of the water.

2. Add the salt, sugar, and cumin and whisk once again.

3. To make the tarka heat the oil to almost smoking point, add the mustard seeds and allow them to sizzle and pop for a few seconds before adding the curry leaves. Remove from the heat and drain the oil away, retaining the mustard seeds and curry leaves to add to the lassi.

4. Finally add the mint leaves, mustard seeds and curry leaves to the lassi. Place it in the fridge and leave to infuse.

5. When you are ready to serve, transfer to a jug and add the ice.

6. Serve cold.

7. Enjoy!

Mango & Mint Coolie

Mint and mangoes are a match made in heaven and probably two of my favourite summertime ingredients. This recipe turns the ripe mangoes into a refreshing cool drink. Like most of the drinks in this chapter this is simple to prepare but is intensely delicious and a lovely way to rehydrate! Depending on the ripeness and sweetness of the mangoes you may be able to reduce the sugar content significantly.

The Indian mango season is celebrated with great enthusiasm as it is an eagerly anticipated event. The Indian Alphonso mangoes are amongst the sweetest and least fibrous mangoes in the world and for this reason I would sooner wait until the Indian mangoes are in season rather than settle for second best.

Serves 4

Ingredients:
2 large mangoes – but 3 or 4 if they are Kesar Indian mangoes since they're smaller
100ml water
5 tbsp. caster sugar (it dissolves more easily)
¼ tsp ground roasted cumin
Pinch of black salt
12 mint leaves
500ml chilled water
Ice cubes

1. Peel and dice the mangoes. Place them in a pan with 100ml water to poach them with 3 tablespoons of the sugar. When softened, set them aside to cool for a while then transfer them to a food processor or hand blender, add the remaining sugar and pulp into a smooth paste. Add the cumin and black salt.

2. Crush half of the mint leaves in a mortar and pestle and add to the mango mix; stir once again.

3. Now add 500ml of chilled water and stir.

4. Transfer to a serving jug and add the ice cubes.

5. Garnish with the remaining mint leaves.

6. Enjoy!

Chef's Tip:
Drop the sugar down to taste – to get more health benefits.

Falooda

As a child I loved the concept of the falooda: milk, ice cream, rose syrup and nuts – what's not to like?! However I actually hated the rose water flavour running through it. Today I'm still not a fan of the rose water but I've come to make a recipe that only carries a small hint of it. Of course you may love the taste of the rose water and so I've included it in the recipe. You could increase the quantity of rose water for a truly authentic flavour. I prefer my recipe.

Serves 4

Ingredients:
2 tsp chia seeds (tukmaria or basil seeds)
150ml cold water
10g fine vermicelli seve or very fine glass noodles
125ml rose syrup
1 litre full fat milk – chilled
4 scoops of good quality vanilla ice cream
Toasted almond flakes and pistachio nuts – to taste

1. Place the chia seeds in a bowl and pour in the cold water. Soak for up to 30 minutes; they will swell up like jelly. Drain and set aside.

2. In the meantime, cook the vermicelli noodles by plunging them into hot water and soaking for a few minutes. Drain the noodles, rinse them in cold water and set aside, or follow the instructions on the side of the packet for the glass noodles.

3. When the chia seeds are ready, begin to assemble the drink: start with the rose syrup by dividing the syrup into the 4 serving glasses, then spoon over the drained chia seeds into the glass, and now distribute the vermicelli.

4. Pour the chilled milk into the glasses followed by a scoop of ice cream. Finish off with a sprinkling of toasted almonds or pistachios.

5. Serve immediately.

Lily Chai Ki Limboo
Lemongrass & Lime Drink

Lemongrass is often referred to as lily chai in Hindi and is used to make herbal tea infusions in India. This is a perfectly refreshing drink and delicious for alfresco afternoons. You could of course add a slug of vodka or Bacardi for a party theme!

Serves 4

Ingredients:
2 heads fresh lemongrass, outer layer removed
4 limes
4 lime leaves
8 tsp caster sugar
Ice cubes, to blend and for decoration
6 fresh mint sprigs
500ml boiling water

To garnish:
2 lemongrass stalks, outer layer removed and quartered lengthways, to give 4 long strips from each stalk

1. Chop 2 lemongrass heads crosswise into 1cm pieces.

2. Finely grate the zest of 1 lime and reserve. Slice off and discard the white pith from the zested lime. Cut the flesh into tiny green dice.

3. Remove the zest of the remaining 3 limes by peeling, using a floating-blade peeler, and reserve the zest. Halve and squeeze the 3 limes for their juice.

4. Put the chopped lemongrass, any shorter zest strips (reserve the long pieces to garnish), 8 ice cubes, the leaves of 2 mint sprigs, the finely grated zest, chopped lime flesh, lime juice and sugar into a blender. Blitz for 30 seconds. Add the 500ml boiling water and stir until the sugar dissolves.

5. Chill for a few hours.

6. When ready to serve, put 6 ice cubes into each tall serving glass. Divide the longer lime zest pieces between the glasses.

7. Strain the liquid through a sieve, pour into the glasses, stir gently and add the remaining mint sprigs and the quartered lemongrass stalks.

Nutritional Tip:
Lemongrass has excellent antioxidant and anti-cancerous properties.

Beetroot & Pomegranate Juice

I'm a big fan of both beetroot and pomegranates and together they become a superfood like no other. Use honey instead of sugar to keep all the health benefits in place or perhaps add a sweet variety of apple to the juice blend instead of the honey.

Serves 4

Ingredients:
2 large pomegranates
200ml water + 50ml water
2-3 beetroots – peeled and quartered
2 inch piece of fresh ginger – sliced
Juice of 1 lemon
2 tbsp. honey
Ice cubes
2-3 mint leaves

1. Deseed the pomegranates and remove the white membrane. Place in a food processor jug with the 200ml water and blitz.

2. Remove the lid and using a fine strainer strain the juice clear of the seeds. Set aside.

3. Now place the beetroot and ginger slices in a NutriBullet or similar blender, add 50ml of water and blitz to a smooth consistency.

4. Remove from the blender and strain through a very fine sieve or muslin cloth, squeezing the beetroot through the cloth to extract as much juice as possible.

5. Transfer to a jug; add the lemon juice, pomegranate juice and honey and stir well.

6. Add the ice cubes.

7. Place the mint leaves on top of one another, roll them up and then slice them thinly into ribbons. Add the mint to the jug.

8. Enjoy soaking up all the goodness of beetroot and pomegranate.

Chef's Tip:

Add celery to the juice to add extra health benefits as well as a slightly salty influence to the flavour.

Spice Blends

Whilst I'm a puritan when it comes to spices, I do like creating spice blends and heavily rely upon my trusted favourites – and not just for Indian cuisine.

Spice blends are as the name suggests – a blend of spices selected for their specific attributes in creating a harmonious flavour. I also like the convenience of having a ready-made set of flavours to choose from and being able to quickly marinate ingredients without having to start from scratch.

In those instances I'm referring to marinades whereas traditional spice blends are components such as garam masala, chaat masala or pau bhaji mix, and each family is likely to have their own unique recipe.

The rules to making and enjoying the best spice blends if you choose to accept them are:

1. Buy fresh spices.

2. Purchase organic and non-radiated spices to ensure the essence of the seed or flower is still intact.

3. Make small quantities and enjoy the flavours and fragrance as fresh as possible.

4. Store in cool dry conditions out of sunlight and in airtight containers.

Here I have shared some of my family recipes for traditional spice blends.

Garam Masala

It was after receiving a gift from my best friend of her mother's homemade blend of garam masala that my love affair with perfecting this spice blend began. I can hardly believe that it was almost 20 years ago!

I've preached about the abuse and overuse of cumin and coriander seeds in commercial recipes so I've veered away from adding them here, instead creating a very pure blend. It is prized for its very even melding of heat, earthy tones and depth of flavours; no spice overpowers another, which is exactly how it should be. I know every blend is a special family heirloom but I was fortunate enough to coax this one out of the recipe vault over some Diwali festivities.

Makes approx. 100g

Ingredients:
12g cloves
17g black peppercorn
5g mace
17g green cardamom – whole pod
17g cinnamon powder or 1 whole cinnamon
12g whole giant black cardamom pods
4 star anise
10g bay leaves
¼ nutmeg, crushed into small pieces then blitzed in the spice grinder

1. Start by placing the big ingredients into a mortar and pestle to break down into smaller pieces that are more manageable. Do this in sections and a few at a time to be more effective.

2. Place all the ingredients into a coffee grinder or dry blender and grind into a fine powder.

3. Store in an airtight, non-clear container, away from direct sunlight.

Chef's Tip:
Make small quantities to keep the blend as fresh as possible.

Chaat Masala

A chaat masala is a hot, sour and salty spice blend that creates that tongue smacking, head shivering sensation when tasted. It adds a certain something to a dish, elevating it even further. It is a staple addition to a great many north Indian street food dishes or salads. The essential and key ingredient is the powerful combination of dried mango powder and black salt and when these are combined with other seeds such as roasted cumin it's a match made in heaven.

Like garam masala, there are many different recipes depending on regional and community preferences. Here is my version that has been in my family and tailored to suit my palate over the years.

Makes approx. 60g

Ingredients:
1 tbsp. black salt
1 tbsp. roasted cumin seeds
1 tbsp. amchoor (mango powder)
2 tsp garam masala
½ tsp asafoetida

1. Place all of the ingredients into a spice or coffee grinder. Grind into a fine powder.

2. Store in an airtight non-clear container away from direct sunlight.

Chef's Tip:
Make small quantities to keep the blend as fresh as possible.

Chai Masala Spice Mix

You have to be an avid Indian tea drinker to appreciate the need for a good chai masala blend. It is as important as the tea leaf you make to brew the tea or arguably even more so. That first cup of tea in the morning made with masala and then the afternoon cuppa is a ritual in itself as well as an addiction, though the masala can be added to a non-caffeinated tea. The notion of non-caffeinated would fall on deaf ears in my family and most others all over the world.

It may seem rather odd to add spices to tea; do Indians have spices with everything? Well, the answer is almost always YES. Since spices are used for their medicinal value, for every ingredient there is a spice that will enhance its effectiveness and ensure it doesn't disturb the chemical balance in the body.

It therefore stands to reason that you can't just add any old spices to make masala chai; the spices selected for tea are ones that stimulate the digestive system and help to break down the lactose enzymes, thus making tea pleasurable and good for you.

Makes approx. 130g

Ingredients:
30g black pepper
30g green cardamom
12g cinnamon bark
12g cloves
50g white pepper
½ tbsp. ground dried ginger powder

1. Place the large ingredients into a mortar and pestle and grind to small pieces in readiness to place in the spice grinder; you don't want to put too much stress on the blades by putting them in whole.

2. Once broken into smaller pieces transfer to the spice grinder. Now add the smaller whole spices to the spice grinder and grind to a fine powder.

3. Finally add the powdered ingredients to the blender, and grind once more to integrate the spices together.

4. Place the accumulated blend into a sterilized dry storage container, preferably metal, to avoid deterioration by the light. Shake well to ensure all the spices have blended evenly into each other once again.

5. Store in a cool dark place – out of sunlight.

6. Enjoy a cup of tea knowing that the spice blend has passed through generations of families and is an old trusted recipe of good pedigree.

Pau Bhaji Masala

This masala was originally created for a pau bhaji recipe; however, I use it for a number of vegetable recipes including mashed aubergine and kidney bean curry. It is robust and delicious and plays well with a host of vegetables, so it seems a shame to re-invent the wheel every time.

Makes approx. 50g

Ingredients:
2 tbsp. coriander seeds
1 tbsp. cumin seeds
2 pods green cardamom
1 black cardamom
6 cloves
2 star anise
1 tsp fennel seeds
1 tsp hot chilli powder
3 tsp Kashmiri chilli powder
½ tbsp. turmeric powder
1 tbsp. dry raw mango powder (amchoor)
1 tsp cinnamon powder
1 tsp ground dry ginger
1 tbsp. garam masala powder
¼ tsp asafoetida
1 tsp salt
½ tsp black pepper

1. Place all of the whole spices into a spice grinder and whizz up into a fine powder.

2. Now add the ground spices and whizz once more to blend.

3. Turn out into a clean sterilized jar and store out of direct sunlight for up to 6 months.

Spice Tip:

Kashmiri chilli powder will give you the wonderful deep red of the chillies without the fierce heat, much like paprika but with a little gentle heat.

Jhaal Muri Spice Blend

Jhaal muri is a popular street food snack in the Kolkata region of India. Jhaal means spices and muri is the very popular puffed rice which is eaten throughout most of India in some form or another. In this recipe the puffed rice is mixed with potato, cucumber and tomatoes. This is a traditional spice blend recipe for jhaal muri, however the blend could easily be used as a marinade with chicken or lamb chops. For a vegetarian option it would pair very well with butternut squash or aubergine. If you are using the blend as a marinade then add 1 tablespoon of oil for every tablespoon of spice blend and use as a rub.

Makes approx. 130g

Ingredients:
30g cumin seeds
15g coriander seeds
10 bay leaves

25g black salt
18g white pepper
18g dried mango powder
15g red chilli powder
12g garam masala

1. Place the cumin seeds, coriander seeds and bay leaves into a spice grinder and blend until they are broken down to a coarse powder.

2. Now add the remaining ingredients and continue to grind until it becomes a fine powder.

3. Decant into a clean airtight jar and store in a cool and dark place.

Panch Poran

Panch poran is essentially the Indian five spice (panch means five in Bengali). It is a blend of aromatic seeds that are often fried in oil or ghee before adding onions or the main ingredients. The tarka process infuses the oil with the aromas of the oils in the seeds and causes them to pop as a result of the heated oil in the pan. Panch poran tends to be used mainly in Bengali recipes, giving a bittersweet and aniseedy flavour to dishes. Unlike many other spice blends panch poran is made up of whole seeds rather than grinding to a powder.

The blend is made of equal parts cumin, fennel, nigella, fenugreek and mustard seeds.

Makes approx. 50g

Ingredients:
3 tsp cumin seeds
3 tsp fennels seeds
3 tsp nigella seeds
3 tsp fenugreek seeds
3 tsp mustard seeds

Place all the seeds into an airtight jar, shake well and store in a cool and dark place.

Eating & Cooking with Your Hands

I remember as a child being embarrassed at the notion of eating with my fingers. I would always eat with cutlery in front of my friends at school for fear of being perceived as uncouth or, worse still, culturally ignorant.

Whilst I eat with my hands at home I am still guarded about this practice. The more upmarket the restaurant, the less likely I am to eat anything with my fingers and even if it takes an age to finish the meal, I'm likely to abandon it before using my hands. That probably explains why I try to refrain from visiting fussy upmarket eateries as the pleasure of enjoying food beats etiquette every time.

Food is meant to be enjoyed and even scientifically speaking, using your hands enhances the eating experience. Taste, texture and smell are all perceived better through our fingers. Your fingers send senses to the brain about the temperature and texture of the food and act like a catalyst in generating the necessary salivary juices.

Fingers are quite simply more nimble; this is equally true in the cooking process, and it's much easier to get a feel of the weight, viscosity and density of the dough or batter mix when you've got your fingers in the bowl, than mixing with a spoon. In cooking, the biochemistry changes with hand temperature. The gentle warmth radiating from your palm helps to bind certain foods together, just as we tend to use fingertips only when making pastry to keep the dough cool whilst the opposite is true for mixing oil with spices in spice blending.

Then there is the alchemy, call it biochemistry; the metal instrument obstructs the instant connection of flavours to the palate. Tasting food from your hand, particularly for seasoning purposes, is really important as the cold metal instrument is an alien texture and temperature to the tongue and roof of your mouth, whereas your fingers are of the same temperature and texture and so there is no downtime in tasting the true flavour of the food.

The Science, Health & Hygiene

We all have some bacteria, known as normal flora, found on our skin. These bacteria are not harmful to humans; instead, they protect us from many harmful bacteria from the outside environment.

It is important to establish normal flora in various parts of our body such as the mouth, throat, intestine and gut for maintaining our health. Eating with a spoon for a long time can change the arrangement of normal flora, which results in reduced immunity to environmental bacterial germs. If you quite like the idea of eating with your hands then here are some rules to follow:

RULES FOR EATING WITH YOUR FINGERS

1. Use only your right hand to eat.

2. The left hand is used to move unwanted food or serve others and yourself fresh food. Using the right hand to then serve others or replenish would be considered 'double dipping' and potentially lead to cross-contamination of saliva.

3. Only your fingers should be used, not the palm as this conveys a messy eater.

4. The thumb of the hand is used to catapult the food into your mouth and is elegant.

5. Don't use all of your fingers; the baby finger is usually left clean.

6. You have to tear the chapatti with one hand but children and novices might use both hands. Using your thumb and fingers to tear a piece of the bread off, scoop the curry or the vegetables with the bread and eat.

7. For the rice, you can use your fingers and thumb to similarly move the food into your mouth. Mix a bit of curry and rice together on the plate to make a little ball, then bring it up to your mouth.

The Role of Vital Vitamins & Minerals

The key ingredients in my recipes are all bursting with health-giving properties, including all the vitamins and minerals that we need to keep us fighting fit.

But it is worthwhile taking the time to understand why these nutrients are important to our physiology at all, and what contribution they make to our overall wellbeing, for instance, what's the significance of vitamin B or vitamin K to our wellbeing in the grand scheme of things? Over the next few pages allow me to shed some light, in a most uncomplicated way. Of course I'm not attempting to cover chapter and verse, simply to give you an idea of food and effect.

VITAMIN A:
Plays an essential role in vision, normal bone growth and the growth of healthy skin and nails. It helps us to fight infection and assists in the digestion of food. Foods high in vitamin A include: most orange and yellow fruit and vegetables, dark green leafy vegetables such as spinach, kale, sweet potato, carrots, squash, pumpkin, cabbage, liver, and fish liver oils, milk products, butter, eggs, black pepper, cloves, cumin, mustard and chillies.

VITAMIN B:
There are eight subcategories of vitamin with the complex B group. These vitamins are essential when it comes to making new blood cells, new DNA cells and certain brain chemicals. Vitamin B also helps us to metabolise protein and carbohydrates correctly, turning food into energy or

fuel. A deficiency in vitamin B can lead to anaemia, fatigue and shortness of breath. You'll find vitamin B1 in peas, spinach, nuts, soya, liver, beef and pork. Vitamin B2 is in okra, asparagus, milk, cheese and eggs. Vitamin B6 is in potatoes, bananas, chicken, turkey, mackerel, mullet and salmon. B12 can be found in dairy products, offal, eggs, beef and seafood.

B-complex – the broad band of B vitamins – are contained in caraway seeds, cumin, mustard, black pepper, turmeric, fennel, and chillies.

VITAMIN C:
Vitamin C is a building block of collagen, which is the structural material for bone, skin, blood vessels and other tissue. If you don't get enough vitamin C, you can suffer from inflamed gums, scaly skin, nose bleeds and painful joints, amongst other ailments. Some research suggests a persistent lack of vitamin C can lead to cancer of the mouth or digestive tract. Foods rich in vitamin C include black pepper, cloves, cayenne, cumin, mustard seeds, turmeric, fennel, green chillies, mustard, greens such as methi spinach, cauliflower, capsicum, cabbage, peas, tomatoes, kiwi fruit, mango, strawberries, broccoli, papaya, oranges and cantaloupe melon, parsley, fresh rosemary, fresh thyme and peas.

VITAMIN D:
Essential for strong and healthy bone development, vitamin D also helps make sure your muscles, heart, lungs and brain work well and that your body can fight infection. Our bodies can make their own vitamin D from sunlight, but if you don't get enough exposure on a daily basis, you can also get vitamin D from supplements. Only

a very small amount of the vitamin D we get comes from the food we eat. A deficiency in vitamin D can make your bones more fragile and lead to other abnormalities like bow legs, but mostly a lack of energy is most evident. We also need vitamin D to absorb calcium from the food we eat. Foods containing vitamin D include almonds, eggs, mushrooms, cod and halibut oils, salmon, tuna and mackerel.

VITAMIN E:
Vitamin E is one of nature's most effective antioxidants and provides protection from lung damage, which can be caused by pollution. Vitamin E and A work together to make red blood cells which support the immune system and there is growing evidence that vitamin E is an effective anti-aging tool, helping the brain fight off diseases like Alzheimer's. Foods high in vitamin E include almonds, tofu, spinach, avocados, shellfish, broccoli and squash.

VITAMIN K:
Vitamin K is essential in enabling the blood to clot, building strong bones and preventing heart disease. It is found in leafy green vegetables and the good bacteria in fermented food. Foods high in vitamin K include broccoli, Brussels sprouts, carrots, spinach, celery, grapes and peas.

ANTIOXIDANTS:
You'll find antioxidants in most of my recipes, and with good reason! Antioxidants are a group of naturally occurring chemicals in fruit and vegetables that protect our blood cells. They are incredibly important in protecting us from the damaging toxins in our atmosphere and other environmental stresses can do. Antioxidants can be found in vitamins A, C and E as well as in copper,

selenium and zinc. Research has revealed that a diet rich in antioxidants such as black pepper, cinnamon, cloves, cumin, mustard, turmeric, fennel, nutmeg, berries, capsicums, mangoes and oranges helps protect us against cancer and heart disease.

BETA & ALPHA-CAROTENE:
Beta-carotene is a red/orange pigment found in many fresh fruits and vegetables, which is converted into vitamin A. We need vitamin A for healthy skin and mucous membranes, our immune system, and good eye health and vision. Beta-carotene is a carotenoid and an antioxidant. It is fat soluble and therefore best consumed with some form of fat. Some evidence suggests that beta-carotene might slow cognitive decline.

Foods rich in beta-carotene include onions, sweet potato, carrots, peas, spinach, lettuce, cantaloupe melon and squash, apricots, and broccoli.

Alpha-carotene is a precursor to creating vitamin A in the body, and while important, is far less common than beta-carotene. Like beta-carotene, alpha-carotene is fat soluble and is best consumed with some form of fat.

Alpha-carotene foods include orange vegetables like pumpkin, carrots, and winter squash. Other alpha-carotene food sources include tomatoes, napa cabbage, Swiss chard, collards, green beans, tangerines, capsicums, bell peppers, and peas.

CALCIUM:
Calcium is essential to healthy teeth and building of strong bones and maintaining bone density. It is a vitamin that needs constant maintenance to ensure there is not loss of bone density and to keep you healthy in old age. Calcium is lost on a daily basis through our skin, hair, nails, sweat, and passage of water and motions. The body does not produce calcium of its own so it is important we get calcium from the food we eat. Calcium can be found in: poppy, celery, fennel, sesame and chai seeds. It can also be found in asafoetida, bay leaves, black pepper, cardamom, cinnamon, cumin, fenugreek seeds and leaf, mace, nutmeg, mustard, star anise, and turmeric. In dairy food calcium is found in hard cheeses especially parmesan, as well as in yoghurt, probiotics and milk. Leafy greens such as spinach and kale as well as figs also contain calcium. Almonds have the highest amount of calcium in nuts. In proteins, canned fish such as salmon as well as tofu and edamame contain protein. Finally amaranth, which is a pseudo cereal, and some lentils also do.

COPPER:
Copper is required in the production of red blood cells. It is a mineral that is found throughout the body and keeps nerve cells and your immune system healthy. It also helps form collagen, a key part of bones and connective tissue. Copper may also act as an antioxidant, reducing free radicals that can damage cells and DNA. Copper can be found in spices such as asafoetida, bay leaves, cumin and coriander seeds, fenugreek seeds, mustard, nutmeg, mace, seafood, organ meats like liver, nuts, legumes, fruits and vegetables.

FIBRE:
Fibre is very important to our wellbeing and gut health. Fibre starts by smoothing out our digestion and enables the absorption of glucose and fats in the small intestine. Fibre provides fuel for 'good'

bacteria in our large intestine which in turn benefit us by making vitamin B12, and releasing fatty acids from the dietary fibre which are important for good colon health.

Fibre is important for good bowel motions that will eliminate toxins. Good motions reduce the risk of cancer and so are essential to our diets. Food rich in fibre includes: ajwain seeds, coriander seeds and plant, cinnamon, cumin seeds, fennel seeds, and turmeric as well as wheat, corn and rice, bran, nuts, seeds and wholegrain foods.

IRON:
Iron is an important component of haemoglobin, the substance in red blood cells that carries oxygen from your lungs to transport it throughout your body. If you don't have enough iron, your body can't make enough healthy oxygen-carrying red blood cells. A lack of red blood cells is called iron deficiency anaemia.

Foods rich in iron include: Asafoetida, bay leaves, cardamom, chilli, cinnamon, cumin and coriander, nutmeg, star anise and fenugreek seeds, as well as spinach, lentils, pumpkin seeds, quinoa, shellfish, red meat, and turkey.

MAGNESIUM:
Magnesium is crucial to nerve transmission, muscle contraction, blood coagulation, energy production, nutrient metabolism and bone and cell formation. Most magnesium is stored in the bones and organs. It is naturally available in many types of food, yet despite this, magnesium deficiency is extremely common. A deficiency in magnesium can have a significant adverse impact on our nervous system, affecting our mood, and leading

to anxiety and insomnia. Magnesium is essential to muscle recovery and repair particularly if you are a very active or sporty person. Foods rich in magnesium include: asafoetida, bay leaves, black pepper, caraway seeds, cinnamon, cloves, coriander, cumin, fenugreek seeds, mace, nutmeg, star anise, almonds, Brazil nuts, walnuts, avocado, beans, wholegrain wheat and rice, leafy greens, spinach, pumpkin seeds, yoghurt, and bananas.

OMEGA-3 FATTY ACIDS:
This is another essential nutrient that has become better known over the last decade. It plays a vital role in bodily functions such as controlling blood clotting and building cell membranes in the brain. As our bodies cannot produce omega-3 fats, we must get them through food. Omega-3 fatty acids are also natural anti-inflammatories and protect against heart disease and possibly strokes. New studies are identifying potential benefits for a wide range of conditions including cancer, inflammatory bowel disease and other auto-immune diseases such as lupus and rheumatoid arthritis. It's easy to think only fish oils are high in omega-3 fatty acids as this is the food commonly mentioned but there are a number of other sources that are important – particularly if you don't eat fish. Foods containing omega-3 are typically rapeseed and vegetable oils, linseeds and walnuts as well as vegetables such as those on the phytochemicals list – kale, broccoli, squashes and of course oily fish such as salmon and mackerel.

PHYTOCHEMICALS:
Phytochemicals are important nutrients that can be found in dark leafy green or orange vegetables such as kale, watercress, spinach and pumpkin. They help to block

the growth of cancerous cells in the body and maintain good long-term health. Studies show that people who include phytochemical rich foods in their diet have a lower incidence of rheumatoid arthritis, cancer and cardiovascular disease.

POLYPHENOLS:
Polyphenols are a large group of chemical compounds found in plants. They are characterized by the presence of more than one nutrient group such as antioxidants, antiseptics, and anti-inflammatory agents. These chemicals are known to neutralise free radicals, reduce inflammation and slow the growth of tumours. Polyphenols help to improve blood vessel function, the metabolic function and thereby improve energy levels.

Polyphenols add astringency and bite to foods. For example you'll notice it in tea that's brewed too strongly (tannins) and in the 'greenish' flavour of extra-virgin olive oil or the back palate of red wine. Anything that makes your mouth pucker generally contains polyphenols.

In plants, polyphenols help defend against attack by insects and give plants their colour (anthocyanins). For example: resveratrol in red wine, capsaicin in chilli and paprika, thymol in thyme, cinnamic acid in cinnamon, rosmarinic acid found in rosemary, thyme, oregano, sage and peppermint. Polyphenols are very important to gut health and wellbeing and so I have outlined some examples of the top foods containing polyphenols by food category.

Spices: cloves, star anise, capers, black pepper, coriander, methi leaves, ginger, cumin, cinnamon.

Dried herbs: peppermint, oregano, sage, rosemary, thyme, basil, lemon verbena, parsley, marjoram.

In vegetables: globe artichokes, red chicory, green chicory, red onion, spinach, broccoli, curly endive.

Dark berries: black chokeberry, black elderberry, low bush blueberry, plum, cherry, blackcurrant, blackberry, strawberry, raspberry, prune, black grapes.

In seeds: linseeds, celery seeds.

In nuts: chestnuts, hazelnuts, pecans, almonds, walnuts.

Green & black olives

Other fruits: apples, apple juice, pomegranate juice, peach, blood orange juice, lemon juice, apricot, and quince.

In oils: extra-virgin olive oil, and rapeseed oil.

POTASSIUM:
Potassium is a mineral which has several important functions in the body, largely regulating fluid levels and nerve and muscle function, including regulating heart rhythm. It is found in all cells in the body, and levels are regulated by the kidneys. It works alongside sodium to maintain a normal blood pressure. Potassium levels will affect our metabolism of foods, thus it is an essential mineral and one that is naturally in many foods. Foods rich in potassium include: bay leaves, black pepper, cardamom, caraway seeds, chillies, cinnamon, cloves, fennel seeds, turmeric, beetroot, black beans, edamame, winter squash, sweet potato, yoghurt, tomato sauce, and watermelon.

ZINC

Zinc is found in cells throughout the body. It is needed for the body's defensive (immune) system to properly work. It plays a role in cell division, cell growth, wound healing, and the breakdown of carbohydrates. Furthermore it is thought to play a role in brain function, helping to keep the brain alert and responsive to learning.

It is also thought to prevent heavy metals from accumulating in the brain, helping to prevent degeneration of cells, and reducing the risk of conditions such as Alzheimer's.

A large quantity of zinc is stored in the eyes. It works together with vitamin A to ensure the health of the retina, helping the eyes to sense light, and reducing risk of certain age-related eye conditions, such as macular degeneration.

Zinc is also needed for the senses of smell and taste – essential if you are a cook or foodie! Foods rich in zinc include: Bay leaves, black pepper, cinnamon, coriander and cumin seeds, fennel, fenugreek seeds, mustard, turmeric, almonds, cashew nuts, chia, pumpkin and squash seeds, chickpeas, lima beans, kidney beans, asparagus, broccoli, courgettes, mushrooms, oats, wheat germ, tofu, pork and lean chicken.

Ailment Alleviators

ANAEMIA:
Aniseed, bay leaves, cumin, celery seeds, fenugreek seeds, sesame seeds, turmeric, parsley. Eat plenty of foods such as: spinach, leafy greens, watercress, kale, kiwi, onions, okra, fish, chicken, liver, eggs, milk, cheese, raisins and dates.

ARTHRITIS:
Cinnamon, black pepper, ajwain and cloves, nutmeg, rosemary, lemongrass. Hot herbs: garlic, ginger, chillies, lemongrass, turmeric. All berries, cherries, broccoli, watercress, mustard, all types, spinach, citrus fruits, seeds (particularly linseed), nuts. Avoid tomatoes and aubergines.

ASTHMA:
Asafoetida, cloves, cinnamon, nutmeg, turmeric, seeds and their oils, Blueberries, celery, cherries, carrots, marjoram, hot herbs (garlic, onion and ginger), sweet potato, watercress, walnuts and fish.

BRAIN POWER (ALZHEIMER'S & COGNITIVE DETERIORATION):
Herbs and spices include: black pepper, cinnamon, clove, saffron, nutmeg, mace, turmeric, ginseng, lemongrass, thyme, sage, oregano, rosemary, holy basil (tulsi), and valerian.

Eat fish oils, all types of seeds and nuts, yoghurt, aubergine.

CARDIOVASCULAR DISEASE:
Allspice, basil, bay leaves, black pepper, caraway seeds, chilli powder, coriander powder and leaf, fenugreek, paprika. Chinese five spice, cinnamon, cloves,

coriander, and cumin. Herbs include: dill, hawthorns, hibiscus, marjoram, mint, rosemary and thyme. Hot herbs include: garlic, ginger, chillies. Eat plenty of omega-3 & 6 foods such as oily fish, salmon, mackerel and sardines. All fruit and vegetables, in particular citrus fruits, celery, onion, cucumber as well as nuts and seeds are essential to good cardiovascular performance.

COLDS AND FLU:

Ajwain, anise, cloves and cinnamon, cardamom, cumin, mace and nutmeg, turmeric, fresh chillies and chilli powder.

Herbs such as: rosemary, sage, thyme, and hot herbs: particularly turmeric, ginger and chillies. Ginger, honey and lemon as well as turmeric with honey linctus are particularly effective. Fruit, especially citrus fruits, all the berries, leafy greens and vegetables.

CONSTIPATION:

Black pepper, bay leaves, cardamom, cinnamon, cloves, cumin, coriander, fennel, fenugreek, ginger, turmeric. Peppermint tea, green tea, clove tea, lemon water. Apples, prunes, rhubarb, mint, linseed, oats, lentils, cucumber, beetroot, celery, chicory, parsley, sage.

DIABETES:

Fresh chillies and chilli powder, cinnamon, cloves, curry leaves, dill seeds, fenugreek, ginseng, turmeric, marjoram, oregano, rosemary, sage, garlic, ginger. All green vegetables and leaves, seeds (particularly sesame) and nuts, eggs, lentils, brown rice and lean meats.

DIGESTION:

Asafoetida, ajwain, black pepper, bay leaves, caraway seeds, cardamom, celery, cinnamon, chilli, cloves, coriander, cumin, curry leaves, dill seeds or dill spinach, fenugreek seeds, fennel, nutmeg and turmeric. Fresh herbs such as basil, chamomile, fresh chillies, garlic, ginger, lemongrass, oregano, rosemary, thyme.

ECZEMA:

Eat foods that are high in essential oils particularly omega-3 fatty acids as well as anti-inflammatories of which turmeric and cinnamon are the most powerful agents known. Eat plenty of cruciferous vegetables such as broccoli, kale, cauliflower, cabbage, as well as foods high in carotenoids – yellow, red and orange fruit and vegetables. For oils – eat oily fish, seafoods, nuts, seeds, particularly linseed, leafy greens, celery, bok choy, spinach, beetroot and probiotics such as sauerkraut, kimchi and kefir. Eat plenty of berries, papaya, pineapple; the chemical bromeline is particular important to skin cells. Avoid dairy foods.

HEARTBURN AND ACIDITY:

Cumin, fennel and dill seeds, fresh fennel, dill, mustard, turmeric, spinach, ginger, cardamom, papaya, bananas and apples. Fish (baked or grilled). Avoid all fried food. More alkaline food should be consumed to balance the body's pH and regulate to about 7 on the scale. Reduction of red meat, poultry, fried food, and dairy from your diet.

HIGH BLOOD PRESSURE:

Basil, cinnamon, cardamom, turmeric, hot herbs: garlic, ginger, onion, and chillies. High fibre foods, all the seeds and their oils, celery, red grapes and cucumber. Less consumption of meat and acidic foods.

INSOMNIA:
Aniseed, cumin, dill seeds, fenugreek, holy basil, nutmeg, poppy seeds, saffron, sesame seeds, valerian, chamomile, parsley, peppermint, sage.

Almonds, apple cider vinegar, bananas, chamomile and herbal tea, boiled eggs, lettuce, jasmine rice, oats, tuna fish and plenty of veggies.

Food rich in carbohydrates stimulates secretion of serotonin and melatonin which induces sleep. Apple, barley, beans, black-eyed peas, blueberry, bran, brown rice, buckwheat, chickpeas, corn, dates, figs, grains, grapes, lentils, macaroni, muesli, pasta, pear, peas, pineapple, potato, raisins, refried beans, rice, strawberry, watermelon, white beans, bread, whole wheat bread, wholegrain cereals.

IBS:
IBS symptoms can vary hugely from person to person but for most people avoid the skin, pith and pips from fruit and vegetables. Eat all cooked vegetables, except perhaps cabbage, cauliflower, and broccoli, which might cause too much gas.

Eat plenty of starchy carbohydrates such as bread, rice, cereals, pasta, potatoes, chapattis and plantain. Eat meat, chicken and fish however avoid oil, spicy and fried foods. Most herbs and spices are digestive aids and will actively help conditions such as IBS. Spices: ajwain, allspice, cardamom, cinnamon, cloves, ginger, mace, nutmeg, peppermint, star anise. Herbs: basil, caraway, fresh and seed coriander, cumin, dill, fennel, fenugreek, marjoram, oregano, paprika, rosemary, thyme, turmeric.

PROLONGED TIREDNESS AND LOW ENERGY:
Cardamom, chilli powder, cinnamon, cloves, coriander, cumin, turmeric, oregano, holy basil, green tea, garlic, ginseng, reishi mushrooms, cacao. Eat high fibre, vitamin C rich, low glycaemic index foods, oats, walnuts, almonds, orange flesh vegetables including pumpkins, squash and sweet potato, maca, mushrooms, dense green leafy vegetables and yoghurt and eggs. Use honey for sweetening where necessary, but cut down overall on sugar.

Table of Essential Vitamins & Minerals in Spices

	Antioxidants	Calcium	Copper	Fibre	Iron	Magnesium	Potassium	Vitamin A	Vitamin B	Vitamin C	Zinc
Asafoetida	✓	✓		✓	✓						
Ajwain	✓			✓							
Bay Leaves		✓	✓		✓	✓	✓				✓
Peppercorn		✓			✓	✓	✓		✓		✓
Caraway Seeds		✓	✓	✓	✓	✓	✓		✓		✓
Cardamom		✓			✓	✓	✓			✓	
Chillies					✓	✓	✓	✓	✓		
Cinnamon	✓	✓			✓	✓	✓				✓
Cloves	✓				✓	✓	✓	✓		✓	
Coriander		✓	✓	✓	✓	✓	✓				✓
Cumin	✓	✓	✓	✓	✓	✓		✓	✓	✓	✓
Fennel	✓	✓	✓	✓	✓	✓	✓		✓	✓	✓
Fenugreek Seeds		✓	✓		✓	✓	✓				✓
Mace		✓	✓		✓	✓					
Mustard	✓	✓	✓		✓			✓	✓	✓	✓
Nutmeg	✓	✓	✓		✓	✓	✓				
Star Anise		✓			✓	✓	✓				
Turmeric	✓	✓		✓	✓	✓	✓		✓	✓	✓
Yams	✓			✓						✓	

Table of Spices by Their Health Properties

	Anaemia	Analgesic	Antimicrobial	Anti-Cancer	Anti-Inflammatory	Antioxidants	Brain Health	Carminative	Constipation	Digestive Stimulant	Immune System
Ajwain			✓								
Allspice		✓	✓		✓			✓		✓	✓
Anise Seed	✓					✓		✓		✓	
Asafoetida								✓	✓	✓	
Bay Leaf	✓			✓				✓			✓
Black Pepper	✓			✓	✓	✓				✓	
Capers				✓		✓					✓
Caraway Seeds	✓	✓		✓				✓		✓	✓
Cardamom						✓		✓	✓	✓	✓
Chillies			✓	✓	✓	✓	✓			✓	✓
Cinnamon			✓	✓	✓		✓	✓		✓	
Clove		✓	✓		✓	✓	✓	✓		✓	
Coriander			✓			✓		✓	✓	✓	✓
Cumin	✓		✓		✓	✓		✓		✓	
Fennel				✓		✓			✓	✓	
Fenugreek	✓			✓		✓		✓		✓	✓
Mace & Nutmeg		✓			✓	✓	✓			✓	✓
Mustard	✓	✓	✓			✓				✓	✓
Turmeric	✓		✓	✓	✓	✓	✓		✓	✓	✓

Table of Essential Vitamins & Minerals in Vegetables

	Antioxidants	Calcium	Copper	Fibre	Iron	Magnesium	Potassium	Vitamin A	Vitamin B	Vitamin C	Zinc
Aubergine	✓			✓		✓	✓		✓	✓	
Bitter Chard	✓			✓	✓	✓	✓	✓		✓	
Broccoli	✓	✓	✓	✓	✓		✓	✓	✓		✓
Cabbage	✓	✓	✓	✓	✓	✓	✓		✓	✓	
Capsicums	✓			✓		✓	✓	✓	✓	✓	
Cauliflower	trace		✓	✓		✓	✓		✓	✓	
Garlic	✓	✓			✓	✓	✓		✓		
Ginger	✓				✓	✓	✓		✓		✓
Green Banana	trace		✓	✓			✓		✓	✓	
Green Beans	✓	✓		✓	✓	✓	✓	✓	✓	✓	✓
Mustard Green	✓			✓			✓	✓	✓	✓	
Okra	✓						✓	✓		✓	
Peas	✓			✓			✓		✓	✓	
Potatoes	✓			✓		✓			✓	✓	
Spinach	✓	✓	✓						✓	✓	
Sweet Potato	✓					✓			✓		✓
Tomatoes	✓	✓	✓	✓	✓	✓		✓	✓	✓	
Turnips	✓	✓		✓		✓			✓		✓
Yams	✓			✓						✓	

Table of Vegetables by Their Health Properties

	Anaemia	Analgesic	Antimicrobial	Anti-Cancer	Anti-Inflammatory	Antioxidants	Brain Health	Carminative	Constipation	Digestive Stimulant	Immune System
Aubergine	✓			✓	✓	✓			✓	✓	✓
Bitter Chard	✓			✓	✓	✓	✓				
Broccoli	✓	✓	✓	✓	✓	✓	✓		✓	✓	✓
Cabbage		✓	✓	✓	✓	✓	✓		✓		✓
Capsicums		✓	✓	✓	✓	✓	✓		✓	✓	✓
Cauliflower			✓	✓	✓	✓	✓		✓		✓
Garlic		✓	✓	✓		✓	✓		✓	✓	✓
Ginger	✓	✓	✓	✓	✓	✓	✓	✓		✓	✓
Green Banana				✓	✓		✓		✓	✓	✓
Green Beans				✓	✓	✓					
Mustard Green					✓	✓	✓		✓		✓
Okra	✓		✓	✓	✓		✓		✓	✓	✓
Peas	✓		✓	✓	✓	✓	✓				✓
Potatoes	✓		✓		✓						✓
Spinach	✓	✓	✓	✓	✓	✓	✓		✓	✓	✓
Sweet Potato			✓	✓	✓	✓	✓		✓	✓	✓
Tomatoes	✓		✓	✓	✓	✓	✓				✓
Turnips	✓	✓	✓	✓	✓	✓			✓		✓
Yams			✓	✓	✓	✓	✓		✓	✓	✓

Weights & Measures

Measuring quantities in cooking is very important, particularly when you are just setting off on the journey of cookery. I recommend you buy a set of measuring spoons for accuracy, particularly with the smaller quantities.

⅛ teaspoon	½g	½ml
¼ teaspoon	1g	1ml
½ teaspoon (tsp)	2.5g	2.5ml
1 teaspoon (tsp)	5g	5ml
½ tablespoon (tbsp)	7.5g	7.5ml
1 tablespoon (tbsp)	15g	15ml

Grams and millilitres are the same weight. If you have a larger quantity you need to measure, you can use your scales to measure the ingredient. Using scales can help you get a more accurate measurement of liquid than you would when using a measuring jug. A set of digital scales is a great investment as these allow you to measure grams or millilitres. By using the 'tare' mode you can put a bowl or jug on the scales, zero the weight of the empty vessel and therefore measure the quantity you need.

When using tinned goods, it is important to check the 'drained weight', particularly for ingredients like beans which are canned in liquid. The tin may say 400g, but the weight of the beans will be only 240g. The tin's label will state the drained weight.

'A pinch of...' is a phrase often seen in recipe books. What does that mean? It is usually the amount of salt or ground pepper you can pick up with your thumb and index finger, which equates to 1/16th of a teaspoon! Fingers and thumbs vary in size, and you may have seen TV chefs using three fingers and their thumb which is very generous. For seasoning, I recommend you start with your index finger and thumb, and taste the dish, adding more seasoning if you think the dish needs it. As you get more confident, you will know how many fingers and thumbs to use for a pinch of salt.

A pinch of herbs is a little different, and on page 39, I explain the three-finger pinch for herbs, which equates to a tablespoon.

Glossary of Terms

ATTA
Milled wheat flour

AYURVEDIC (AYUR = LIFE, VEDA = SCIENCE)
Ayurveda is the study of life science in the literal sense. It is a traditional Hindu practice of medicine dating back thousands of years which is based on the idea of balancing the body chemistry through diet. The mind and body are entirely related to each other and mindfulness about what you eat according to your body chemistry is the key to good health.

BHEL PURI
Thin plain wheat flour biscuits usually fried to the consistency of a crispbread and used in chaat recipes.

CAPSICUM
Commonly known as peppers, related to chillies but with no heat.

CHAI SEEDS
Edible seed of Salvia Hispanic, a flowering plant in the mint family, with health benefits.

DAAL/DAL
Lentils

DARIOLE MOULD
Small flower pot shaped metal mould in which individual sweet or savoury dish is set, baked or cooked.

GELATINE
A colourless, water soluble protein used for setting jellies. It is derived from meat or fish bones and can come in leaf and powder form and different strengths (always read the manufacturer's instructions).

GHEE
Clarified butter (see page 40)

GRAM FLOUR
Ground chickpea flour

HDL
High-density lipoproteins, so called "good cholesterol".

IDLI
Steam rice cakes – usually eaten with sambaar.

JAGGERY
Unrefined pure cane sugar (see page 55).

JULIENNE
Very thinly sliced/shredded vegetable.

KARAHI
A flat bottomed wok, traditionally made out of cast iron, now available in stainless steel or non-stick materials.

LDL
Low-density lipoproteins, so-called 'bad cholesterol'.

MAIDA
Highly refined wheat flour without any bran.

MASALA DABBA
Traditional spice tin with 7 round spice tins and tightly fitting lids.

MORTAR & PESTLE
Stone bowl (mortar) and long stone with a rounded end (pestle) used to grind spices.

MURI
Indian puffed rice

PANEER
Indian cottage cheese

PATLI
Board to roll chapattis, parathas and puris.

RDA
Recommended Daily Amount

ROUX
Equal quantities of butter and flour cooked together and used to thicken a sauce.

SAMBAAR
A lentil and vegetable broth made from 'toor' lentils. Often poured over idli or eaten as an accompaniment with dosas.

TAMARIND PASTE
Tamarind is a reddish-brown pod-like fruit that contains a sweet-sour tasting pulp which is used in many dishes and chutneys.

TARKA
Whole spices are infused in hot oil or fat to release their essence and transfer the spice to the oil.

TARKA PAN
A small cooking vessel designed to reduce the splashing out of seeds during a tarka process.

TAWA
Bevelled or flat cast iron cooking griddle for chapattis or parathas.

TUKMARIA SEEDS
Chia seeds

UMAMI
A savoury taste

URAD/URID DAL BLACK/WHITE
A small lentil with a black shell and white bean.

VAGHAR
Whole spices are infused in hot oil or fat to release their essence and transfer the spice to the oil.

WHELAN – INDIAN ROLLING PIN
A thin bevelled rolling pin used for rolling Indian breads such as chapatti.

Index